What the Flock Do I Feed my Parrot?

By

Lisa Morrison

ABOUT THE AUTHOR

Lisa Morrison is qualified and highly experienced in parrot studies and behaviour. She is a full member of the International Society of Animal Professionals. Lisa has spent years researching, working, and caring for a variety of animals, specialising in parrots and wild birds. Having volunteered and worked with many animal and bird sanctuaries, wildlife parks as well as veterinary clinics, she has gained a wealth of knowledge on the preservation and conservation of birds and wildlife.

Born and raised in a National Park in Southern Africa, Lisa has spent most of her life surrounded by animals. Therefore, it was only natural for her to choose a career path that included them. Being a parrot owner herself, with a lifelong fascination, passion, and love for birds, she has written this book to share her knowledge and vast experience of parrot care and parrot nutrition. This nutritional guide helps parrot owners to provide the best nutrition for their birds to enable them to live long, happy and healthy lives.

DISCLAIMER

This book is designed to provide helpful information on the subject's addressed. The information contained in this book are based upon the research and personal experience of the author. The author has made every effort to ensure that the information in this book was accurate at the time of publishing.

The author of this book is not a qualified avian veterinarian nor a qualified avian nutritionist. The suggestions for addressing specific problems are for informational purposes only and are not intended to diagnose, treat, prevent, and cure any disease. It is not intended to replace competent medical and nutritional advice or treatment by a qualified avian veterinarian or avian nutritional expert. No one should engage in activities beyond their training or expertise. The author is not liable for any loss, damage or injury including death. It is the pet owner's full responsibility to seek veterinary medical treatment in the event of illness or medical emergency. It is the owner's full responsibility to seek professional advice pertaining to their bird's nutritional needs.

This book is not species specific; it provides practical advice on a broad range of topics of parrot nutrition. Each parrot species requires their own unique nutritional supplementation, therefore, this should be discussed with an avian veterinarian or other qualified healthcare provider.

All rights reserved. No part of this book maybe be used or reproduced in any manner whatsoever without the written permission of the author.

Copyright © 2020 Lisa Morrison

DEDICATION PAGE

I dedicate this book to my husband, family, and all my pets present and past.

I first and foremost want to thank God my heavenly father. Being born with a complicated heart condition and surviving two major open-heart surgeries, it is only through his grace and mercy, I am here today, to write this book and share my knowledge.

I want to thank my entire family for all of their love, support and for always encouraging me in everything I do.

I want to thank Delia Crouse for taking the time to proofread my book. I also want to thank Bluewave publishing for doing such an amazing job on the formatting and front cover of this book.

And lastly, I want to thank all my pets present and past, for their unconditional love and for being the reason I wake up each morning with a smile on my face.

Table of Contents

- *CHAPTER 1* 1
  - SAFE FOODS 1
  - SAFE VEGETABLES 1
  - SAFE FRUIT 2
  - SAFE NUTS 3
  - SAFE TABLE FOODS 3
  - SAFE SEEDS 4
  - SAFE TREATS 4
- *CHAPTER 2* 5
  - SAFE HERBS & SPICES 5
  - TIPS ON HOW YOU MAY ADDITIONALLY USE SOME SPICES 6
  - AND SUPPLEMENTS 6
- *CHAPTER 3* 8
  - EDIBLE PLANTS, PLANT SAFETY 8
  - PLANT ENRICHMENT AND POPULAR TOXIC PLANTS 8
  - PLANT SAFTEY 8
  - PLANT ENRICHMENT 9
  - POPULAR TOXIC PLANTS 10
- *CHAPTER 4* 11
  - SAFE WOODS & PREPARING WOODEN PERCHES 11
- *CHAPTER 5* 12
  - TOXIC FOODS, DANGERS OF SALT AND SUGAR 12
  - TEFLON, SAFE COOKWARE & DANGERS IN THE KITCHEN 12
  - SUGAR AND SALT WARNING 14
  - TEFLON, SAFE COOKWARE AND DANGERS IN THE KITCHEN 15
  - SAFE COOKWARE 16
  - DANGERS IN THE KITCHEN 16
- *CHAPTER 6* 17
  - DIETARY SOURCES OF VITAMINS AND MINERALS 17
  - AND THE IMPORTANCE OF THEM. 17
  - VITAMINS A and C 17
  - VITAMIN B 18
  - VITAMIN D 18
  - VITAMIN E 19

- VITAMIN K 19
- VITAMINS IN HERBS 20
- CALCIUM RICH FOODS 20
- THE IMPORTANCE OF CALCUIM 21
- HYPOCALCEMIA 21
- THE IMPORTANCE OF VITAMIN A 22
- HYPOVITAMINOSIS A 22
- VITAMINS IN WATER 23
- VITAMIN TOXICITY (OVER-DOSE) 23
- THE IMPORTANCE OF PROTEIN 25
- THE IMPORTANCE OF WATER 26
- NUTRITIOUS FRUIT AND VEGETABLES TO FEED 27
- FRUIT 27
- VEGETABLES 29

CHAPTER 7 .... *31*
- PESTICIDES, FOOD PREPARATION HYGIENE 31
- AND STORING FOOD 31
- HOMEMADE CLEANER 31
- FOOD PREPERATION HYGIENE 32
- STORING FOOD 32
- THE IMPORTANCE OF REMOVING 33
- OLD FOOD FROM CAGES 33

CHAPTER 8 .... *34*
- INTRODUCING NEW FOODS AND FEEDING PELLETS 34
- INTRODUCING NEW FOODS 34
- BASIC FOODS TO START OFFERING FIRST 34
- WAYS TO INTRODUCE NEW FOODS 35
- A FEW TRICKS TO ENTICE YOUR BIRDS TO TRY NEW FOOD 36
- PELLETS 37

CHAPTER 9 .... *38*
- FOOD ALLERGIES 38
- AND SIGNS OF MALNUTRITION 38
- FOOD ALLERGIES 38

SIGNS OF MALNUTRTION *39*
CHAPTER 10 .... *40*

DELICIOUS RECIPES, CHOPS, MASHES, SMOOTHIES 40
SNACKS, BREEDING FOODS, WEANING FOODS, AND IMMUNE SYSTEM BOOSTING FOOD 40
PICKY EATER RECIPES 41
HIDDEN PELLET RECIPES 46
SUMMER FUN RECIPES... 48
WINTER MASHES 52
A PARROT'S PARTY 54
FOODS FOR BREEDING BIRDS 59
WEANING FOODS... 60
FEATHERIFFIC FOOD 61
IMMUNE SYSTEM BOOSTING FOODS 62
FOODS TO FEED DURING MOULTING AND FEATHER PLUCKING PERIODS 63
FOOD IDEAS FOR ELDERLY PARROTS... 64
FEEDING A SICK BIRD 65
PARROT FEEDING MYTHS DEBUNKED 65
SPROUTING FOR PARROTS 69
SOAKING AND SPROUTING GUIDELINES 70

WHAT THE FLOCK DO I FEED MY PARROT?

CHAPTER 1

SAFE FOODS

SAFE VEGETABLES

Wash all vegetables thoroughly with clean water before consumption.

- Asparagus **(WARNING: This has been reported to cause gastrointestinal upset in some birds, speak to your vet before feeding)**
- Alfalfa
- Artichoke
- Baby corn
- Broccoli
- Beets
- Bell peppers
- Bok choy
- Butternut **(Cooked)**
- Brussel sprouts
- Carrots
- Chilli peppers
- Carrot tops
- Cabbage
- Corn
- Courgettes
- Chard
- Collard greens
- Cauliflower
- Celery **(Remove string)**
- Cucumbers
- Dandelion greens
- Dark green lettuces
- Kale
- Radish
- Parsnip
- Peas
- Pea shoots
- Rocket
- Runner beans **(Remove string)**
- Pumpkin
- Parsnip
- Sweet peppers
- Sugar snaps **(Remove string)**
- Squash **(All types)**
- Spinach
- Sweet potatoes **(Cooked)**
- Turnips
- Watercress
- Yams

SAFE FRUIT

Wash all fruit thoroughly with clean water before consumption.

- Apple **(Remove seeds)**
- Apricot **(Remove pip)**
- Banana
- Blackberry
- Blood orange **(Remove seeds)**
- Blueberry
- Cantaloupe melon **(Seeds are safe to feed)**
- Cherry **(Remove pip)**
- Cranberry
- Coconut
- Dates **(Dried)**
- Elderberry
- Figs **(raw)**
- Gooseberries
- Grapes
- Guava
- Honey dew melon **(Seeds are safe to feed)**
- Kiwifruit **(Peeled)**
- Lychee **(Peeled)**
- Mandarin **(Peeled)**
- Mango **(Remove pip)**
- Nectarine **(Remove seeds)**
- Orange **(Remove seeds, feed on occasion as very acidic)**
- Papaya **(Seeds safe to eat)**
- Passion fruit
- Peach **(Remove pip)**
- Pear **(Remove seeds)**
- Pineapple **(Peeled, feed on occasion as very acidic)**
- Plums **(Remove pip)**
- Pomegranate **(Don't feed skin)**
- Quince
- Raspberry
- Red currents
- Strawberry
- Tangerine **(Remove seeds)**
- Watermelon **(Seeds are safe to feed)**

SAFE NUTS

Please remember to open all nuts with shells to check for mould!

- Almonds
- Brazil nuts
- Cashews
- Hazelnuts
- Macadamia
- Pecan
- Pine nuts
- Pistachio
- Walnuts

SAFE TABLE FOODS

Please take note of which foods need to be cooked!

- Brown rice (Cooked)
- Whole grain rice cakes (Unsalted)
- Whole grain bread (Toasted)
- Oats (Steel cut oats are best to offer -serve cooked)
- Barley (Cooked)
- Whole grain pasta (Cooked)
- Dried beans (Well cooked)- NEVER FEED RAW BEANS THEY ARE TOXIC.
- Potatoes (Cooked)
- Cottage cheese (Parrots are lactose intolerant, therefore, feed dairy products such as cottage cheese which are lactose-free)
- Eggs (Cooked)- NEVER FEED RAW EGG! WHEN BOILING EGGS; BOIL FOR ABOUT 30 MINUTES TO KILL ANY BACTERIA FROM THE CHICKEN.
- Chicken (Well cooked, feed the whites of roasted chicken)- NEVER FEED FRIED CHICKEN AS IT CONTAINS TOO HIGH LEVELS OF FAT.
- Whitefish (Well cooked)- NEVER FEED SHELLFISH AS THE BACTERIA CONTENT CAN BE HARMFUL TO YOUR BIRDS.
- Meat (Well cooked, and in small quantities)-NEVER FEED RAW MEAT OR MEAT THAT HAS BEEN RE-HEATED.

SAFE SEEDS

- Anise seeds
- Cantaloupe seeds
- Caraway seeds
- Cardamom seeds
- Chia seeds
- Coriander seeds
- Cumin seeds
- Fennel seeds
- Flax seeds
- Grape seeds
- Melon seeds
- Milk thistle seeds
- Papaya seeds
- Passion seeds
- Pepper seeds
- Pomegranate seeds
- Poppy seeds
- Pumpkin seeds
- Sesame seeds
- Squash seeds

SAFE TREATS

- Animal crackers
- Homemade oven baked corn tortilla strips **(Do not add salt)**
- Madeira cake
- Millet
- Nutriberries
- Pet shop treats made for pet birds
- Plain Cheerios
- Plain corn flakes
- Plain digestive biscuit
- Plain rice Krispies
- Plain rich tea biscuit
- Plain unsalted/unsweet popcorn
- Shredded wheat
- Unsalted crackers
- Unsalted pretzels

(Morrison, 2020, PG 110-115)

CHAPTER 2

SAFE HERBS & SPICES

Introduce new herbs slowly into the diet and feed in very small quantities. If herbs are not offered in moderation it may affect your bird's digestive system. Do not use medicinal herbs alongside conventional medications without consulting with your avian vet first, as some can interfere with certain medications.

- Alfalfa
- Aloe Vera
- Anise **(Leaves and seeds)**
- Basil
- Bay leaf
- Cayenne
- Celery root
- Chamomile
- Chickweed
- Chicory
- Cinnamon
- Cloves
- Coriander
- Dandelion
- Dill
- Eyebright
- Fennel
- Ginger
- Lavender
- Lemon balm
- Lemongrass
- Milk thistle
- Mint
- Nettle
- Oregano
- Parsley **(Feed in moderation)**
- Rosemary
- Sage
- Slippery elm
- St John's wort
- Star anise seeds **(Pod)**
- Thai basil
- Thyme
- Turmeric root

TIPS ON HOW YOU MAY ADDITIONALLY USE SOME SPICES AND SUPPLEMENTS

Many herbs and spices can be extremely potent and have side effects of which the owner may not be aware which can prove fatal for the parrot. Use herbs and spices in moderation and always consult with your avian vet before using them.

CAYENNE PEPPER- Rich in vitamin **A, C, E, B,** is a must have in any parrot household. It can be used to help stop external bleeding. If your parrot has a cut sprinkling some on the wound helps the blood to clot quite quickly. It has natural antifungal and antibacterial properties. It can also be used as a natural pain relief which can be sprinkled over food. The raw or powdered form has to be used in order for it to be effective. Bear in mind, this is a natural pain relief, so may not bring great comfort to a bird in chronic pain. If your bird is in pain, seek veterinarian help immediately.

PAPRIKA- Rich in vitamins **A, B, C, E & K** is a natural antibacterial, antioxidant and anti-inflammatory. It aids digestion and can help reduce inflammation with ailments such as arthritis. Ensure you check the ingredients label, as many other spices are often added to it. It should only list paprika as sole ingredient.

TURMERIC- This spice has amazing properties: anti- cancer, anti-tumour, antibacterial, antifungal, anti-inflammatory, antiparasitic, antibiotic, immunostimulant, lowers blood pressure, natural painkiller, antioxidant, antiviral, natural liver detoxifier, antiseptic. It can be used to disinfect cuts and it speeds up the healing process. This spice can be added to birdie bread, as well as sprinkled on soft food or mixed in with live yogurt.

Note: Turmeric does act as an anti-coagulant (prevents blood clotting at the normal rate) therefore, inform your vet before blood tests. Do not feed it while birds are moulting or suffer with blood feather issues.

CINNAMON- ONLY USE CEYLON CINNAMON! Other varieties can cause liver damage; if you are not 100% certain its Ceylon cinnamon, then do not buy it. Ceylon cinnamon has anti-inflammatory, antifungal, antimicrobial and antiviral properties. It can help boost the immune system and lower blood sugar.

BLACK PEPPER- A good source of minerals: potassium, calcium, zinc and manganese, vitamin B_6, thiamine, riboflavin and niacin. It is an Anti-inflammatory, antispasmodic and antibacterial. It helps to stimulate the immune and digestive system. It can also be used to help with clotting; apply black pepper on a cut and it will help stop the bleeding quiet quickly.
Use sparingly, in whole and freshly ground form, not in the powdered form.

ALOE VERA- This has been used for centuries and has antiseptic, antibacterial, anti-inflammatory and analgesic properties. You can safely use it on minor cuts and burns to help speed up the healing process. It contains numerous vitamins and minerals when taken orally. Pure aloe vera juice can be added to food and water in a ratio of one-part aloe juice to 3-parts water. Always read the label first as some brands may contain additives and stabilisers which can be very harmful to your birds. **Check first with your avian vet before giving aloe vera orally. Many people spray it on their bird's feathers, especially, feather plucking parrots. However, it should ONLY be sprayed on bare skin and not on the feathers themselves; a build-up on the feathers causes a sticky residue to form resulting in the birds not being able to insulate themselves.**

CUTTLEBONE and MINERAL BLOCKS- These two supplements should always be present in your bird's cage. Cuttlebone adds calcium to your bird's diet and mineral blocks are especially important for birds such as budgies which are prone to iodine deficiency.

PROBIOTICS- Probiotics are great for digestion and have many health benefits. They are especially important to be given after a bird has been on a long dose of antibiotics to replace the good gut bacteria lost. You can choose from many avian probiotics on the market. Ask your vet which one will be best for your bird.

CHAPTER 3

EDIBLE PLANTS, PLANT SAFETY
PLANT ENRICHMENT AND POPULAR TOXIC PLANTS

Just because a plant is edible does not necessarily mean they should be fed to your bird as part of their balanced diet; it simply means that if your birds were to eat them, they would be safe to sample. Consult with your avian vet first before adding plants into your birds' diet.

Below, are a few popular plants believed to be safe for parrots:

- Aloe Vera
- African violets
- Bottlebrush
- Bamboo
- Bougainvillea
- Buddleia
- Camomile
- Chrysanthemum
- Dandelion
- Echinacea
- Elderberry flowers
- Fuchsia
- Hibiscus
- Nasturtium
- Pansy
- Red clover
- Rosehips
- Rosemary
- Roses (**Remove thorns**)
- Spider plant

PLANT SAFTEY

Do not feed your birds plants that you have purchased from florists, garden centres, shops or picked from the side of the road. These flowers will be laced with insecticides and many other chemicals that can kill your birds. Only give your birds flowers which you have grown yourself at home or acquired from a source that can guarantee they are chemical free and safe to feed.

PLANT ENRICHMENT

Always double check with your avian vet before feeding your birds any types of plants.

Fuchsia- (All varieties) plants are a great source of enrichment for parrots. Lories and Lorikeets will love the pollen it produces.

Nasturtium- (*Tropaeolum*) safe for humans and parrots to eat; parrots will have hours of fun chewing the leaves, stems and seed pods.

Buddleia- (*Buddleja davidii*) parrots will love these and all parts are safe for them to eat.

Roses- only give the heads; the thorns on the stalks can cause injury. Ensure they have not been treated with chemicals.

Elderflowers- are a great enrichment and a fantastic source of vitamin C.

Dandelions- all parts are safe for birds. However, ensure they have not been treated with chemicals.

Sunflowers- sunflower heads will keep your birds entertained for hours. The seeds are packed with vitamins and minerals. However, feed sunflower seeds in moderation.

Rosehip- is high in vitamin C and helps to maintain liver and kidney function.

Hibiscus flower- helps to reduce blood pressure and support heart health and is a favourite of many parrots.

Chamomile flower- has natural calming properties and parrots love them.

Pansy flower- are rich in antioxidants properties and look gorgeous in a chop.

POPULAR TOXIC PLANTS

There are a few popular plants which are found in the home at certain times of the year, such as anniversaries, Christmas, and Valentine's day. However, some of these plants can be deadly to birds.

I have listed below a few popular plants which should be kept out of your birds reach:

- **Christmas trees-** these are often sprayed with pesticides, herbicides and fungicides throughout their life cycle. Many owners allow their parrots to play and chew on Christmas trees, sadly, poisoning themselves at the same time. Keep birds away from the Christmas trees. Alternately, make their own safe wooden trees, hanging safe treats and toys.
- **Mistletoe-** the leaves and the berries are toxic to parrots.
- **Holly-** is toxic to parrots.
- **Morning glory-** is toxic to parrots.
- **Various types of lilies-** is toxic to parrots.
- **Daffodils-** are highly toxic to parrots.
- **Poinsettia-** are highly toxic to parrots and other pets.
- **Poppy-** is toxic to parrots.
- **Roses-** while roses are not toxic to parrots, they are frequently sprayed with pesticides that can be fatal. Offer roses which are home-grown and have not been treated with chemicals.
- **Amaryllis-** are popular flowers and look gorgeous in the home, however the whole plant is toxic to parrots.
- **Ivy-** is highly toxic to parrots.
- **Lilies-** however gorgeous and often make up many bouquets, they are toxic to birds.
- **Morning glory-** beautiful on the kitchen windowsill, unfortunately toxic to parrots.
- **Shamrock-** won't bring much luck to your birds or any of your pets. They are highly toxic to all pets.

CHAPTER 4

SAFE WOODS & PREPARING WOODEN PERCHES

In the list below, I've named a few natural woods which are reportedly safe to use for perches. Thoroughly wash and disinfect all wood. Ensure the tree is free from pesticides and all other chemicals before use. Remove all mould.

- Almond
- Apple
- Ash
- Bamboo
- Beech
- Bottle brush
- Cactus wood
- Citrus
- Dogwood
- Elm
- Fir
- Grape vine
- Hazelnut
- Lilac
- Mulberry
- Nut trees
- Palm
- Papaya
- Pear
- Pussy willow
- Rose
- Sycamore
- Willow
- Yucca

PREPARING WOOD FOR USE:
Wash and scrub the wood thoroughly with soap and water, removing all mould, fungi, and bacteria. Disinfect with an avian safe disinfectant and rinse thoroughly. Dry in the sun or bake in the oven at 250F.

QUICK TIP: NEW VINYL FLOORING
Parrots have experienced severe breathing difficulties when placed in a room with newly laid vinyl flooring. One lady gave an account of nearly losing both her birds due the toxic smell. Allow the room to completely air out for a few days before placing your birds in that living area.

CHAPTER 5

TOXIC FOODS, DANGERS OF SALT AND SUGAR
TEFLON, SAFE COOKWARE & DANGERS IN THE KITCHEN

In the list below, I have listed toxic foods which should NEVER be fed to a parrot. Always check whether a new food is safe before feeding it. If in doubt consult with your avian vet. The word "Toxic" does not mean it is bad for you, it means it is poisonous.

- Alcohol
- All carbonated soft drinks
- Apple seeds
- Asparagus
- Avocado
- Caffeine
- Chocolate
- Dairy products
- Dog and cat food
- Dried fruit
- Egg plant
- Fruit pits
- Garlic
- Human medication
- Junk food
- Mushrooms
- Olives
- Onions
- Peanuts
- Raw/dried beans
- Rhubarb
- Street drugs
- Tobacco
- Tomato-steams and vines

- **Alcohol** – the tiniest amount can be fatal. Under no circumstances should a bird be given alcohol.
- **All carbonated drinks-** are high in sugar, preservatives, caffeine and artificial colouring. It also contains carbon dioxide gas. Never give your birds carbonated drinks.
- **Apple seeds-** contain cyanide.
- **Asparagus-** there have been many reports of it causing digestive upset in birds. **Speak to your vet before feeding it.**
- **Avocado-** can prove fatal. Both skin and the pit can cause cardiac distress and heart failure in birds. **Never ever feed your bird avocado.**

- **Caffeine-** can prove fatal. It can cause cardiac malfunction, arrhythmia cardiac arrest and death.
- **Chocolate-** can prove fatal. It can cause diarrhoea, vomiting and effect the bird's central nervous system; which in turn, can cause seizures and death. Keep all chocolate and candy away from birds.
- **Dairy products-** parrots are lactose intolerant which can cause digestive issues.
- **Dog and cat food-** should never be fed to your birds for several reasons. A few of the main reasons is that pet food is often bought in large bags, therefore, the likelihood of mould spores present is high, ingesting these spores may cause severe illness in a parrot. Dog and cat food often contain too-high concentrations of chemicals in relation to the size of a bird's body, thus causing a toxic reaction to occur. Dog and cat kibble can be too hard or too large for birds to eat, resulting in them choking.
- **Dried fruit-** shop bought dried fruit often contains the preservative sulphur dioxide which can cause severe allergic reactions. Homemade dehydrated fruit is safer to feed, however, feed in moderation because of the high sugar content.
- **Eggplant-** the leaves and steams are part of the nightshade family and are toxic to parrots. Eggplant can cause terrible digestive issues so do not feed it to your birds.
- **Fruit pits-** contains cyanide.
- **Garlic-** contains Allicin which can cause anaemia.
- **Human medication-** should never be given to a bird, unless instructed to by an avian vet. Human medication can cause severe allergic reactions, internal bleeding and death.
- **Junk food-** is high in fat, sugar, salt, artificial colourings and preservatives. It is detrimental to a bird's overall health and can cause obesity. Many preservatives found in human food can cause severe allergic reactions in birds. Sadly, numerous birds have needed emergency medical treatment, and many have died from salt toxicity when fed junk food.

- **Mushrooms-** are a fungus and can cause digestive issues. Certain types of mushrooms such as the capped and steamed mushrooms can cause liver failure.
- **Olives-** contain high levels of sodium and are toxic to parrots.
- **Onions-** should never be fed to birds. Onions can cause diarrhoea, vomiting and digestive issues. Prolonged use can cause Haemolytic anaemia, respiratory distress, and cause death.
- **Peanuts-** contain mycotoxins and aflatoxins which can cause liver damage, cancers, respiratory disease and Aspergillosis. (Parrots are up to two hundred times more sensitive to aflatoxins than humans.)
- **Raw dried beans-** contain a toxin called Phytohemagglutinin which can only be removed by soaking and cooking. Feeding raw beans can be fatal.
- **Rhubarb-** the vegetable and the leaves have high levels of Oxalic acid and is toxic to birds.
- **Street drugs-** Almost always fatal to birds and other animals. Without question, it is classed as animal cruelty to give street drugs to any animal.
- **Tobacco-** is toxic to birds due to their highly sensitive respiratory system.
- **Tomatoes-** the leaves, stems and vines are highly toxic to birds. The fruit itself can be fed; however, it is acidic and can cause digestive issues and ulcers. **Feed in moderation.**

<u>SUGAR AND SALT WARNING</u>

SUGAR:

Too much sugar in a birds' diet can be extremely detrimental to their overall health. It can lead to obesity, heart disease, yeast infections, diabetes, gout, hyperactivity, nervous disorders, and cancer. Sugar can influence behavioural issues such as: feather plucking, anxiety, irritability, depression and many more. Always check the labels of food products before feeding it to your birds. Foods containing sucrose, corn sugar and corn syrup are refined sugars and should be avoided.

SALT:

To put into perspective just how little salt is needed to cause toxicity, three potatoes crisps for a small bird such as a budgie or cockatiel would be equivalent to **one teaspoon** of salt to a human! Therefore, it does not take much salt to cause damage to a bird's body. Too much salt can cause electrolyte imbalance leading to excessing thirst, dehydration, kidney damage and death.

TEFLON, SAFE COOKWARE AND DANGERS IN THE KITCHEN

"Teflon" is a brand name that many parrot owners look out for. However, there are many brand names which use non-stick surfaces containing PTFE which is highly toxic to parrots. PTFE fumes cause irreversible lung damage and death. It can kill a bird in just a few minutes. The "non-stick" coating possibilities these days are nearly endless, therefore, always check the labels before using any equipment in a home with birds.

Listed below are a few household items which are Teflon "non-stick" coated:

- All "non-stick" cookware/bakeware
- Bake in the bag foods
- Bread machines
- Ceramic cooking stoves
- Cheese moulds
- Clothes irons
- Coffee maker
- Cookie sheets
- Electric skillets
- Fast-food containers
- Food wraps
- Hair curlers
- Hair straighteners
- Hairdryers
- Ironing board covers
- Pizza machines
- Popcorn bags
- Popcorn makers
- Self-cleaning ovens.
- Some carpet cleaners
- Some heat lamps
- Some light bulbs
- Some microwave dishes
- Some pet bowls
- Waffle makers
- Woks

SAFE COOKWARE

Always use safe cookware alternatives if birds are present in your home.

Below is a list of safe cookware alternatives parrot owners can use:

- Cast iron
- Ceramic (Beware some ceramic cookware has non-stick surfaces, so read the label)
- Copper
- Copper-clad stainless steel
- Glass
- Stainless steel

DANGERS IN THE KITCHEN

The kitchen is a very dangerous place for a parrot to hang out in. There are multiple hidden dangers such as: hot stoves, open pots of food cooking, boiling water and oil, steam, fumes from cooking oils, smoke, fumes from heated oven surfaces, kitchen sink full of standing water, uncovered bowls of oil, knives and other sharp cutlery, food, spices and cleaning solutions which may be toxic to parrots. The bird can wander into open ovens, fridges, cupboards, microwaves and washing machines; they may also get trapped behind these items unbeknown to the owner. Kitchens are busy areas, and the owner may accidentally stand on their bird, or accidentally knock their birds in open pots. The list of potential dangers in the kitchen are endless. **Therefore, birds should be kept out of the kitchen at all times.**

CHAPTER 6

DIETARY SOURCES OF VITAMINS AND MINERALS AND THE IMPORTANCE OF THEM.

The lists below contain essential vitamins and minerals required for a healthy bird's diet, including their dietary sources. Also, you will learn 'why' certain vitamins and minerals are essential for a parrot's health, along with the dangers of over supplementing their diet. Additionally, I have listed some foods which hold 'high nutritional value', therefore, should not be omitted from a bird's diet.

Check food preparation of each food source FIRST before feeding it to your birds. (You'll find this information in Chapter One of this book).

VITAMINS A and C

- Acai berry
- Apple
- Apricots
- Banana
- Bell pepper
- Bok choy
- Broccoli
- Brussel sprouts
- Butternut-squash
- Cantaloupe
- Carrots
- Cherries
- Chili pepper
- Courgette
- Cucumber
- Dandelions
- Dried dates
- Fennel
- Figs/raw
- Gooseberries
- Grapefruit
- Green beans
- Guava
- Kale
- Okra
- Papaya
- Peas
- Pumpkin
- Rocket
- Romaine lettuce
- Spinach
- Sweet potatoes
- Turnip greens
- Watercress
- Winter - squashes- **(A)**
- Yams

VITAMIN B

- Acai berry- **(B1, B2, B3)**
- Almonds - **(B1)**
- Apple- **(B, B2, B6)**
- Artichoke- **(B12, B6)**
- Banana- **(B6)**
- Bell pepper- **(B6)**
- Blueberry- **(B6)**
- Bok choy- **(B6)**
- Brazil nuts- **(B1)**
- Broccoli- **(B5, B6)**
- Brussel sprouts- **(B1)**
- Butternut squash- **(B6)**
- Cantaloupe melon- **(B6)**
- Cauliflower- **(B6)**
- Chilli pepper- **(B6)**
- Courgette- **(B6)**
- Cranberry- **(B6)**
- Cucumber- **(B)**
- Dandelion leaves- **(B6)**
- Date-**(B3)**
- Fennel- **(B6)**
- Fig- **(B6)**
- Grapefruit- **(B6)**
- Green peas- **(B1)**
- Kale- **(B6)**
- Okra- **(B6)**
- Peas- **(B6)**
- Pecan halves- **(B1)**
- Radish- **(B6)**
- Sesame seeds- **(B1)**
- Spinach- **(B6)**
- Sunflower seeds- **(B1)**
- Sweet potatoes- **(B1, B2, B6)**
- Swish chard- **(B2)**
- Turnip greens- **(B6)**

VITAMIN D

- Beef liver- **(cooked)**
- Eggs- **(cooked)**
- Cloves
- Cucumber
- Most Kellogg's cereals

VITAMIN E

- Almonds
- Apricot
- Blackberry
- Blueberry
- Brussel sprouts
- Butternut squash
- Cranberry
- Dried dates
- Eggs
- Kale
- Kiwi
- Mulberry
- Palm fruit
- Plum
- Pumpkin
- Raspberry
- Swiss chard
- Turnip greens
- Walnuts

VITAMIN K

- Apple
- Apricot
- Artichoke
- Blackberry
- Blueberry
- Bok choy
- Broccoli
- Brussel sprouts
- Cabbage
- Carrots
- Cauliflower
- Cheese
- Cherries
- Cranberry
- Cucumber
- Grape
- Green beans
- Kale
- Kiwi
- Leafy greens
- Melon
- Mulberry
- Palm fruit
- Pear
- Plum
- Pomegranate
- Raspberry
- Red currents
- Rocket
- Spinach
- Strawberries
- Swiss chard
- Turnip greens
- Turnip greens
- Watercress

VITAMINS IN HERBS

- Basil- (A, K, C)
- Chamomile- (A)
- Cloves- (C, A, K, D)
- Coriander- (A, K, C, E)
- Dill- (A, C)
- Lavender- (Calcium)
- Mint- (A, C)

- Oregano- (K, A)
- Parsley- (K, C, A)
- Rosemary- (C, A)
- Sage- (A, C)
- Star anise- (C, A)
- Thyme- (C, A)

CALCIUM RICH FOODS

- Almonds
- Apricots
- Black beans
- Bok choy
- Broccoli
- Chickpeas
- Chinese cabbage
- Collards
- Cuttlebone
- Dandelion
- Dried figs
- Flaxseed
- Kale
- Kidney beans

- Mustard greens
- Mint
- Okra
- Oranges
- Pinto beans
- Pumpkin seeds
- Sesame seeds
- Soybeans
- Spinach
- Strawberries
- Tofu
- Walnuts
- Watercress
- Yogurt

THE IMPORTANCE OF CALCUIM

Cuttlefish is often the only source of calcium in many parrot households. Cuttlefish is of course a great source of calcium. However, it may not be enough to prevent many ailments caused by calcium deficiency, especially if the birds are not receiving adequate sunshine (Vitamin D3). Birds need vitamin D3 for calcium absorption.

Calcium is extremely important in a parrot's diet; it is needed for bone formation, muscle function, brain function and nerve function. Breeding birds need it to prevent infertility, becoming egg bound and producing soft eggshells.

It is important that calcium rich foods are included in a bird's daily diet. Calcium supplements are especially important for breeding birds and to help prevent egg binding and soft eggshells. An article entitled "Cuttlefish bone is not enough" featured in the Parrots magazine (issue 268) Rosemary Low, advices to add a calcium supplement daily to rearing food for birds with chicks and for hens, two-three weeks prior to laying a clutch.

Always speak to your avian vet first before supplementing your bird's diet. Too much of a good thing can be detrimental to a bird's health too; diet, age, species and sex of the bird has to be taken into consideration before you use supplements.

HYPOCALCEMIA

Hypocalcemia means lack of calcium (calcium deficiency) it is extremely important for parrots to receive the correct amount of calcium in their diet. If this is not done, they can develop a whole host of medical issues.

Listed below are a few symptoms of Hypocalcemia:

- Bone deformities
- Convulsions
- Egg binding
- Incoordination
- Increased bleeding
- Infertility
- Paralysis
- Perosis
- Poor plumage
- Reduced egg production
- Reduced hatchability
- Retarded growth

- Rickets
- Soft eggshells
- Weakness

THE IMPORTANCE OF VITAMIN A

Hypovitaminosis A means lack of vitamin A (Vitamin A deficiency). Birds which are fed on an all-seed diet alone will lack vitamin A. This is highly detrimental to their overall health and wellbeing. Without venturing into great scientific detail, the reason why vitamin A is essential in a parrot's diet is because it is needed for: the growth and repair of tissues, hearing, eye function, bones, and mucous membranes. Furthermore, without this vitamin the bird will be open to many nasty illnesses, making them vulnerable to fungal, viral and bacterial infections.

HYPOVITAMINOSIS A

As I mentioned earlier in this book, Vitamin A is essential for many functions in a bird's body, without it they will be susceptible to many infections, etc.

Listed below are a few symptoms of Hypovitaminosis A:

- Bone deformities
- Decreased immunity
- Nasal/ ocular discharge and lesions
- Night blindness
- Poor plumage
- Reduced egg production
- Reduced hatchability
- Retarded growth
- Skin lesions
- Soft eggshells

Symptoms of vitamin A deficiency may not show immediately, however, may manifest gradually over several week and even months. Symptoms include increased or excessive sneezing, nasal discharge, ocular discharge, weakness, lack of appetite, wheezing, nasal blockage, diarrhoea, depression, weight loss, swollen eyes and poor feather quality. If you notice any of these clinical signs, see your vet as soon as possible.

The good news is vitamin A deficiency is 100% avoidable; all it takes is for the owner to offer a healthy well-balanced diet to their birds.

VITAMINS IN WATER

Some parrot owners purchase pet shop vitamins which require mixing in with the bird's drinking water. Unfortunately, this method can cause dehydration in birds; many will not touch their drinking water if they can taste something foreign in it. Vitamins lose their potency fast in water, it also speeds up the bacterial growth in the water. Therefore, it is safer to add the vitamins to soft food which will be completely consumed by the bird. Always speak to your avian vet before you supplement your bird's diet.

VITAMIN TOXICITY (OVER-DOSE)

You may have heard the phrase "Everything in moderation" this means too much of anything, even a good thing, can be bad. While vitamins are essential in a bird's diet, **a vitamin "over-dose"** can cause more harm to the bird and the side effects be more severe than an under-dose.

This list is a guide ONLY. I have listed some vitamins and their potential side effects if vitamin toxicity (over-dose) occurs.

Vitamin A

- Crusting of the eyelids
- Decreased bone strength
- Decreased food intake
- Dermatitis
- Haemorrhaging
- Hepatopathy
- Inflammation of the mouth

- Inflammation of the nares(nostrils)
- Swelling of the eyelids
- Weight loss

Vitamin B3

- Decreased PTH
- Hypercalcemia
- Increased bone resorption
- Increased calcium absorption
- Mineralisation of soft tissue
- Nephrocalcemia (excess calcium in the kidneys)
- Polyuria

Vitamin E

- Anaemia
- Decreased bone mineralisation
- Decreased growth
- Decreased liver storage of Vitamin A
- Increased blood clotting time

Vitamin K

- Anaemia
- High mortality
- Hyperbilirubinemia

Calcium

- Decreased food intake
- Hypercalcemia
- Hypophosphotemia
- Nephrosis
- Renal gout
- Visceral gout

THE IMPORTANCE OF PROTEIN

Proteins are extremely important in a parrot's diet and are the building blocks of the body. Proteins are involved in many biological functions of the body such as muscles, feathers, skin, organs and cell membranes. Metabolically, they form enzymes, hormones and immune antibodies. They are also needed for almost all chemical processes in the body such as blood clotting, healing, growth, oxygen transport and water regulation.

Proteins come from different sources: vegetables, animals, and insects. Proteins are made up of amino acids. There are 20 amino acids; 12 of these are called **"Essential amino acids"** because they cannot be made in the bird's body and must be supplied in the diet. **The correct protein balance in a bird's diet is highly essential, without it, illness will follow.**

Let us look at what can happen if parrots receive "too little" protein:

1. Lethargy
2. Poor growth
3. Poor healing
4. Poor plumage
5. Weight loss

Let us look at what can happen if parrots receive "too much" protein:

1. Bone abnormalities
2. Bowel problems
3. Insulation problems (cold intolerance)
4. Kidney damage
5. Poor growth

NOTE: Protein requirements do vary among different species. Speak first to your avian vet about your individual parrot's diet before making any changes.

THE IMPORTANCE OF WATER

Did you know that a bird can lose almost all its body fat and body protein and live? However, if it loses more than a tenth of its body water it will die! Approximately 75% of a bird's body is made up of water. Water is responsible for many biological functions in the body: it is needed to flush out waste, to transport nutrients throughout the body and to regulate body temperature. Without it the bird's blood volume will drop resulting in the liver, kidneys and heart not functioning correctly. Fresh water should be given to our birds daily and should be changed periodically throughout the day.

Bacteria in water doubles every two to three hours. If a bird poops or drops food in their water dish it should be refreshed as soon as it is noticed. If this is not done the water turns into a bacterial soup, resulting in the birds becoming very sick. **The safest water to feed a bird is boiled water regardless of the water source. (Always allow the water to return to room temperature before offering it).**

NOTE: Birds that are fed on pellets will naturally drink more regularly because pellets are so dry. Therefore, water should be always available (of course if you notice your bird drinking excessively, this should be brought to a vet's attention straight away) **Fresh clean water should be available at all times for all species of birds and regardless of diet.**

NUTRITIOUS FRUIT AND VEGETABLES TO FEED

It is important to feed our birds a **wide variety** of fruit and vegetables daily. However, there are some which carry higher nutritional value than others and provide more substantial health benefits.

Listed below are a few fruit and vegetables which are highly nutritious and important to include in a parrot's diet:

FRUIT

Apples- The quote "An apple a day keeps the doctor away" is very true as apples are very nutritious. Apples are rich in antioxidants. They contain fibre, vitamin A, C, K, B7, potassium and iodine. Research has shown that apples are healthy for the heart as they lower cholesterol. **Thread a slice of apple through the cage bars for small birds or cut into chucks for large birds.** (Seeds need to be removed).

Bananas- have the highest protein content than any other readily available fruit; they are also rich in potassium, fibre, vitamin B6, vitamin C and antioxidants. Chop up well for small birds or cut the fruit into grip size pieces with skin on for large birds to hold in their feet. (Many parrots won't eat it if offered over-ripe).

Blueberries- are low in calories, high in antioxidants, help regulate blood sugar whilst containing beneficial soluble fibre and minerals. Offer them whole to large birds or cut in half for small birds. My parrots keep occupied by picking them apart and love their sweet taste. I have personally found that my birds prefer the 'sweet and juicy' variety stated on the label, opposed to the 'aromatic' variety stated on the label. To me, they taste the same. However, my birds do know the difference and will not eat the latter!

Figs- Dried figs are very high in calcium. Figs are rich in potassium, magnesium, iron and copper. They contain vitamin A and K are a good source of antioxidants. **As they are so high in iron and natural sugars, they should be fed in moderation.** Buy good quality dried figs; many poor-quality ones are too dry and not touched. You can feed them dry. However, soak for birds such as Lories.

Kiwi- is rich in antioxidants; it provides a good source of fibre and helps to aid digestion. Kiwi contains vitamin C, K, E, folate and potassium. It boosts the immune system and helps to lower blood pressure. The seeds are edible. Peel the fruit and chop it up or just cut in half and offer to small and large parrots. I use it as a boredom breaker for my birds; they sit there for an hour or so delicately picking out each individual tiny seed.

Mango- is loved by many species of parrot. It is low in calories and high in nutrients. Mangos are high in vitamin A and C and contains valuable minerals. This fruit improves the immune system and aids digestive health, as well as eyesight. Chop it up for small birds or large birds can have a single side removed and they will then eat the inside.

Pomegranate- named as one of the healthiest fruits on earth! What is there not to love about this fruit? It is sweet and juicy, makes a salad or any dish for that matter look fit for a king, and above all it is loaded with antioxidants, vitamins, and minerals. It has potent anti-inflammatory properties which helps with arthritis, joint pain and many other ailments. It helps the body fight against cancer, lowers blood pressure and cholesterol. It has anti-bacterial, anti-fungal and antiviral properties. The seeds of course are edible; however, the skin is not and should not be offered. Remove the seeds and place with other favourite fruits or give as a juice or in a smoothie. This fruit makes a lot of mess and stains badly. If your birds are as messy as mine are, feed away from walls and carpets, as it is guaranteed that the juicy will be sprayed everywhere when they bite into the seeds.

Raspberries- are low in calories and rich in nutrients and vitamins. They contain vitamin A, B, C, E, K, calcium and zinc, etc. They are a great source of fibre and help lower blood sugar. Raspberries have potent antioxidants and anti-inflammatory properties which helps the body fight cancer and many other ailments. It also has anti-aging effects on the body. Offer chopped or whole, juiced or in a smoothie to large and small birds.

VEGETABLES

Beetroot- is an amazing, yet very messy vegetable to feed our birds. It offers antiaging, anti-inflammatory, antioxidant, vascular- protective effects. It is high in vitamin C, minerals and potassium. It helps to manage cardiovascular diseases, reduces blood pressure and lowers inflammation. Feed in slices or chunks to large birds and chop it for small birds. Beetroot juice may also be enjoyed. It is very messy and stains like red wine, therefore, keep away from walls and carpets.

Broccoli- is highly nutritious and a fantastic starter vegetable because birds enjoy picking at the tiny florets. I am sure you will be as surprised as I was to learn from author Rosemary Low that broccoli has more than double the protein found in a sirloin steak, contains more fibre than a slice of whole wheat bread and provides more calcium than a glass of milk. (Low, 2012, PG 35) Broccoli helps reduce inflammation, helps to control blood sugar and boosts the immune system. It is a good source of vitamins A, C and K. Feed raw or steamed, thread through the cage bars, hang on a pet safe skewer or chop it up. My birds go crazy for the "Long steamed" broccoli. I personally find it easier to thread through the cage bars and noticed the taste is sweeter, hence why my birds probably love it.

Carrots- can be found in almost all supermarkets and are inexpensive, yet highly nutritious. It provides birds with carotene which is then converted to vitamin A in the liver. Carotene improves the colour of a parrot's plumage making red and orange feathers vibrant.
Carrots are a great source of beta carotene, fibre, Vitamin K1, potassium and antioxidants. They help to reduce the risk of cancer, improves eyesight, cholesterol and digestion.

Feed raw or par-boiled or boiled. Offer chopped up, cut into sticks or grated. **Do not over feed carrots as it can cause liver issues.**

Courgette (Zucchini)- is high in vitamin A which helps to improve the immune system. It is high in antioxidants and carotene. It contains soluble and insoluble fibre which promotes good digestive health. It also helps reduce blood sugar and heart disease. Feed raw or steamed, chopped up or hang on a pet safe skewer.

Peas, green- are high in nutrients, fibre and antioxidants. They contain vitamin A, C and K as well as many minerals. Peas are a great source of protein. Feed steamed or raw, in or out of the pod. **Remove the string of the pod to prevent choking.** My birds love peas and spend a great deal of time sitting hulling them; they are a great boredom breaker. (**FYI-** Goldfish love peas; it is great for their digestive health and helps with buoyancy issues. (Par-boil the peas and **remove the shell,** cut up into tiny pieces and toss in the tank).

Sweet potato- is a highly nutritious vegetable, rich in vitamins, minerals, fibre antioxidants and beta-carotene. It contains vitamins A, B, C and E, calcium, potassium and beta-carotene. You can feed raw or cooked. Birds love cooked sweet potatoes served warm; it makes a wonderful starter veg for parrots just weaning onto vegetables. It is loved by breeding birds when served warm and fantastic to feed sick and elderly parrots.

Chillies- are rich in many vitamins and minerals, particularly, in vitamin C which is a powerful antioxidant and is needed for a healthy immune system. Parrots do not feel the heat of the chilli due to having fewer taste buds compared to humans. Chillies are a wonderful addition to add to a parrot's diet and can encourage parrots to try new foods if it chopped on top. Large parrots will eat the whole chilli in their feet; chop up for smaller birds.

CHAPTER 7

PESTICIDES, FOOD PREPARATION HYGIENE AND STORING FOOD

According to Pesticide action network UK, pesticides (insecticides, herbicides, fungicides) are not only applied while the produce is growing but can be applied to the seeds and post-harvest too. Additionally, some food items may contain the residue of only one type of pesticide. However, others may contain the residue of multiple pesticides *(this is a scary thought!).* To make matters worse, there are two different forms of pesticides in non-organic produce. The first form of pesticide, the residue sits on the outside of food, the second form are systemic chemicals which are actually absorbed into the food. Unfortunately, no amount of washing or peeling will remove these toxic chemicals. Surprisingly, not even with the use of an expensive vegetable soap.

How must fruits and vegetables be washed to remove pesticides? According to an article written by author Leslie Moran in the Parrots Magazine (Issue 270) the best cleaner is homemade. Researchers found the best and the most simplistic method was to soak the food for 15 minutes in a mixture of baking soda and water. They found that this was the most effective at removing pesticides on and inside the apples which they were testing. Leslie Moran's advices that when you do have to buy non-organic produce, it is important to pick the foods with the lowest pesticide levels, then use the homemade mixture to soak and clean them thoroughly.

HOMEMADE CLEANER

1-part baking soda to 100 parts water
This is ... 1 ounce (1/8 cup or 2 heaped tablespoons) to 12 cups water.

And in metric... 10 grams baking soda to 1 L water.
Let fresh fruit or vegetables soak for 15 minutes. (Moran, Parrot magazine, issue 270, 2020, PG. 17)

FOOD PREPERATION HYGIENE

All surfaces and utensils used to prepare your birds food should be cleaned and disinfected before and after ever use. Always wash your hands thoroughly before preparing food; then dry them on a **disposable paper towel** or on a **freshly laundered** tea towel. Gloves should be used when preparing food, especially, if you are preparing food for chicks **(their immune system is not fully developed)**. Check all food is **safe** to feed your bird before offering it.

All food should be fresh and in date **(check expiry dates)**. Carefully look for mould and bruising. If you do notice mouldy bits, do not just cut them away and think it will be safe to feed; **mould and fungi spread microscopic roots not visible to the naked eye, and can be as harmful as the mould itself.** Fruit and vegetables should be washed thoroughly before feeding it to your birds.

STORING FOOD

This may seem like a boring subject to learn about. However, it is important to know for the health of a parrot. Food that has become stale, mouldy or rancid can cause many digestive issues and even death. If food is not stored in the correct way it loses its nutrients; not only will the birds not benefit nutritionally, hard-earned money would be wasted.

Always check food packaging for the food storing instructions. Temperature plays a vital role when storing food; too much heat or humidity can cause mould and fungi growth, resulting in the food becoming rancid and inedible.

The smell of food is often a good indicator that it has become inedible; stale, musty, sour or putrid odours are a good tell-tale sign that the food should be thrown away. However, some foods contaminated with food- poisoning bacteria may not always have a look, smell, or a taste hence why storing food correctly is essential.

Seeds and pellets should be stored in a cool, dry environment. Such foods should be kept in airtight **glass** containers, and off the ground away from vermin. Some parrot owners purchase large amounts food at one time, unfortunately, by the time they reach the bottom of the bag the nutrients in the food has deteriorated and needs to be binned. This should be avoided. **Do you know that vitamins become completely unusable when left in sunlight; store them in a cool, dark environment.**

THE IMPORTANCE OF REMOVING OLD FOOD FROM CAGES

It is important that ALL old and uneaten food is removed from cages and aviaries daily. Not only does old food attract flies, rats and many other pests, the mould and fungi growth on the food can make your birds very ill and even cause death.
Aspergillosis is caused by a species of mould 'Aspergillus'. You can find it on mouldy food and mould from dirty damp cages. It is a nasty illness and can be very difficult to treat. If caught in the later stages can be fatal; this is one fungal infection you want to avoid at all costs.

Cooked food should be removed after a few hours to avoid the risk of food poisoning, mould and fungi growth which can be fatal.

Many newbie bird owners will over-fill seed cups fearing their birds will run out of food, or it may be due to laziness! This method of feeding is dangerous because the owner may not realise their birds have eaten all the seeds and only the empty husks remain. Left unchanged for days, their birds are slowly starving to death. Furthermore, seeds do go rancid when left out in the open after a length of time. They become inedible and start to grow mould and fungus. Only feed enough food for each day. **FRESH food and water should be given daily.**

CHAPTER 8

INTRODUCING NEW FOODS AND FEEDING PELLETS

INTRODUCING NEW FOODS

If a parrot is not fed on a well-balanced nutritional diet, they are going to suffer from many health issues. Vets all around the world have found that many of the avian illnesses they come across have stemmed from or are a direct result of malnutrition. Birds that live on seed diets alone, fed nothing but sunflower seeds and peanuts, are suffering in silence. So, it is up to the owner to do everything they can to offer the correct foods to keep these birds healthy and happy.

You may have read this phrase in many parrot books; **PERSISTENCE IS THE KEY TO SUCCES.** It is drilled into parrot owners because it is one thing, if not the only thing, which truly works! One cannot offer their bird a vegetable inconsistently and then gives up trying when the bird does not sample it. All too often this manner of feeding is often followed with the excuse, "My bird hates veggies." **The vegetable should be offered every single day, in multiple different ways until that bird eats it, regardless of how long it takes. This is the only way you are going to get that bird to eat it. A bird will not eat something which is unfamiliar, period.**

BASIC FOODS TO START OFFERING FIRST

Start with vegetables which will peak the bird's interest. Broccoli can be pushed through the cage bars; it has tiny florets which will entice the bird to pick at it. Carrots are brightly coloured and can be offered raw or cooked; it can also be presented in many interesting ways, such as in strips, grated, chopped, in spirals or added into other favourite foods.
An apple is a tasty fruit which most birds will try before any other fruit; this too can be cut into slices and pushed through the cage bars. Vegetable mashes,

such as sweet potatoes and butternut squash are relished when fed warm. Newly weaned chicks will sample it as it resembles either formula or their mother's regurgitation. Adult birds will enjoy the warm temperature, and it is easy to add many favourites into the mashes. Mixed leaves such as spinach, kale and chard are great fun for birds; many will bath in them or have fun shredding them. These mixed leaves are highly nutritious. You can place them on the cage floor, hang them up or push through the cage bars.

WAYS TO INTRODUCE NEW FOODS

There are multiple ways in which you can present the food such as chop it, hang it, thread it, place in foraging toys, place it on the cage floor to encourage foraging behaviour, conceal it within other food, eat it yourself. If your bird has a close bond to you and sees you eating, it will likely want what you have. Lastly, many birds learn to eat new foods by watching the other flock members, a monkey-see-monkey-do situation.

It is helpful to know the feeding habits and lifestyle of your pet bird's species in the wild. Learn what foods they eat in the wild, how they eat their food, how often they eat, what times of day they forage for food and how they search for food. With this important knowledge you can mimic their behaviour in the wild, which will help you tremendously. Armed with this information, you will be able to offer foods in such a way the bird will be more inclined to try it and receive enrichment from it.

A FEW TRICKS TO ENTICE YOUR BIRDS TO TRY NEW FOOD

There are a few tricks you can try too, which may help you to get your bird to try new foods, such as placing the food next to a favourite toy, positioning the food on a well-used perch, placing the food next to their staple diet, sprinkling the staple diet on top of the new food. Each time the bird samples the new food gives loads of praise.

Whenever I want my flock to try a new food, I place it inside and outside their cage. I find my birds are more inclined to sample new food while they are out the cage playing on their parrot play station (T-perch). Some birds are afraid of the food. If you feel this is the case, attach it to the outside of the cage instead. Out of curiosity, and the fact it does not appear that intimidating outside their territory, they are often more inclined to try it.

As I mentioned above, eating the food yourself will entice your bird to try the new food. Birds quickly learn what and what not to eat by watching their parents and the rest of their flock. Making facial expressions and sounds of enjoyment will show your bird that what you are eating is not only safe, but tasty too. I will sit next to my bird's cage or next to their T-perch and eat whatever I want them to sample, before long they are climbing on my plate trying to grab bits of food or begging to come out the cage to eat with me. Parrots are social feeders; therefore, this is a perfect opportunity to get them to eat those vegetables. **Never feed birds food straight out of your mouth. This is one of the quickest ways a bird can get sick as their bodies find it hard to fight off the bacteria in our mouths.**

BONUS TIP: Offer the food in a variety of ways simultaneously to see which method they prefer. For example, grab some broccoli and chop it up; then place some on the cage floor for foraging. Take another piece and thread it through the cage bars or hang a piece on an animal safe skewer. Lastly, place some in a foraging toy. Whichever method grabs their attention first, is the one to use consistently for a few days until the bird eats it. I personally find that some days my birds will forage, while other days they prefer to eat the hanging food. It is all trial and error.

PELLETS

Organic pellets are best to feed parrots. Coloured pellets are often full of additives and preservatives. The dyes can change the colour of the bird's droppings giving a false reading resulting in the owner not being able to watch for first signs of illness.

When you first introduce pellets, feed the smallest pellet you can buy regardless of the parrot's species. This method tricks the bird into thinking they are eating seed, and hopefully, they will get a taste for them.

The introduction to pellets should be done slowly and safely over several weeks, even months; done too quickly, and the bird can run into many health issues. Before you transition a bird from a seed-based diet onto a pelleted-based diet a wellness check with a vet must be done first. This is a vital step that should never be missed. A vet will record the bird's weight and do a physical exam to ensure it is in a good physical state to change diet. Changing diet is extremely stressful and can cause any underlying conditions to manifest themselves. The bird's weight must be recorded throughout the switch.

The safest way to convert a parrot onto a pelleted diet is by offering the bird 50% seed and 50% pellets. When you notice that the bird is actually eating the pellets, **slowly** reduce the amount of seed. Once left with 10% seed, stop there and give the remainder as part of your bird's diet; unless specified otherwise by your avian vet.

Never withhold food from your bird in order for them to eat the pellets; it is naïve to assume they will become so hungry they will eat anything. A parrot will not eat food which is foreign to them, they will rather starve to death than eat it. Sadly, this has happened too many times over the years.

CHAPTER 9

FOOD ALLERGIES AND SIGNS OF MALNUTRITION

FOOD ALLERGIES

Yes, birds can suffer from allergies just as much as humans. Parrots can have allergic reactions to food, pollen, moulds, dust and chemicals. Unfortunately, birds react to allergies in multiple ways, often making it very difficult to tell if it is an allergic reaction or an illness. Parrots may react to a food allergy by scratching and itching their skin, feather plucking, screaming, irritability and often aggressive behaviour, while others may become depressed and show no interest in daily activities.

Some foods which may cause a parrot to have an allergic reaction include peanuts, wheat, corn, soy, eggs, flavourings, additives (colouring) preservatives and sulphates. You may be able to find which food is causing the allergy by elimination. Cut out each individual food one at a time and see if there are any changes. **If you suspect your bird is having an allergic reaction or if you notice any of the above symptoms your vet needs to investigate the cause. As I mentioned above, these clinical signs can also be caused by an illness. A vet may be able to test your bird for allergies and give you advice accordingly.**

SIGNS OF MALNUTRTION

Malnutrition is the number one cause of disease and premature death of pet birds today. Do you know one of the five freedoms of an animal quotes: **"Freedom from hunger and thirst by ready access to fresh water and diet to maintain health and vigour. This must be specific to the animal."** (Animal humane society, 2020)

To be able to maintain health and vigour a parrot has to be fed on a well-balanced nutritional diet. A parrot which is fed on a seed-only diet or a pellet-only diet, will suffer from malnutrition and run into many health issues.

I have listed below a few signs of malnutrition. This list is not exhaustive. These symptoms should be taken very seriously. See an avian vet as soon as possible when observed.

- Dry and/or itchy skin
- Overgrown beak and nails
- Scaly, flaky, patchy feet
- Cere has scabs, crusts, scales or flaky appearance.
- Dull, faded, brittle, frayed, damaged, discoloured feathers.
- Stress bars on feathers
- Sinusitis
- Excess sneezing
- Air sacculitis
- Aspergillosis
- Enteritis
- Hepatitis
- Pancreatitis
- Fatty tumours
- Fatty liver disease
- Obesity
- Heart disease
- Feather plucking
- Hormonal imbalanced
- Disproportionally large head
- Skeletal deformities
- White or yellow plaques in the mouth.
- Blunted choanal papillae
- Bald spots while moulting
- Asymmetrical moulting

CHAPTER 10

DELICIOUS RECIPES, CHOPS, MASHES, SMOOTHIES SNACKS, BREEDING FOODS, WEANING FOODS, AND IMMUNE SYSTEM BOOSTING FOOD

In this chapter I will be sharing some amazing easy to make recipes which I have tried and tested over the years. I have included recipes which will help you to introduce new foods and pellets, as well as some delicious treats. I am sure every beak-full will be relished.

During a parrot's life they may go through many stages such as breeding, weaning, stress, moulting, ill health, and old age. Therefore, I have listed foods which can help facilitate their nutritional needs during these periods. You will find these guidelines at the end of this chapter.

Many of the recipes will state to adjust ingredients and quantities as required; this is done with the intention that no food is wasted (one cannot offer a macaw the same size portion as a budgie). You can freeze many of the recipes, however, some owners prefer not to freeze their bird's food. You can also change the ingredients according to produce availability, as well as any special dietary requirements.

TOP TIP: I highly recommend that sprouts are additionally added to every mash and chop recipe. While they may not be mentioned in some of the recipes provided, they add texture, flavour and additional nutrients.

NOTE: These recipes are NOT species specific. Some species of parrot may require vitamins, minerals, protein, calcium, and fats. Some species may need additional supplements in their diet. Speak to your avian vet about the dietary needs for your individual bird.

PICKY EATER RECIPES

Often the best way to introduce new food is by hiding it. Listed below are a few recipes which have hidden fruit and veggies inside, as well as starter chops. Once the bird gets a taste for these new foods you can then start introducing a wider variety. Start introducing foods which are sensitive on the bird's digestive system, such as broccoli, carrots, peas, apple, eggs, brown rice, spinach, and sweet potato.

VEGGIE DELIGHT I START MY DAY RIGHT SQUARES

Ingredients:
1 tsp baking powder
1 free-range egg
½ cup chucky organic apple sauce
½ cup natural organic apple juice
1/3 cup raw broccoli
1/3 cup grated carrots
1/3 cup cooked brown rice
1/3 cup human grade walnuts finely chopped

Preheat oven to 350 °f
Mix all the ingredients together and add the apple juice as needed. Place the mixture in a greased 8x8 pan and pop in the oven for 35-45 minutes. Remove when the stick comes out clean. Cut into squares and serve when cool. You can freeze these.

STARTER CHOP THAT WON'T FLOP

Ingredients: (Adjust ingredients as required)
Finely chop broccoli and baby spinach leaves. Add cooked small shell pasta (conchigliette) finely chopped par-boiled carrots, par-boiled sweetcorn and sprouted seed. Mix all together. Sprinkle seed, pellets or millet florets on top.

Don't leave in the cage more than one to two hours.

SPICY EGGY BREAD

Ingredients:
Eggs, whole wheat bread, organic extra virgin cold pressed coconut oil.

Dip the bread in the egg; ensure both sides are covered in egg. Fry on both sides using the coconut oil in a pan until golden.

Allow to cool and serve warm. You can sprinkle a little cayenne pepper on top.

Do not leave in the cage more than one to two hours.

CHEEKY CHICKEN

Ingredients: (Adjust ingredients as required)
Well cooked (boiled) chicken breast, cooked brown rice, microgreens and sprouted mung beans.

Cook rice as directed on the box. Cut or tear the chicken breast into thin strips. Mix the chicken and the sprouted mung beans into the rice and add the microgreens as a garnish. Serve warm.

Note: Do not reheat this dish. Remove from cage after an hour.

SWEET AND SOUR KABOB

Ingredients: (Adjust ingredients as required)
Broccoli, piece of well-cooked chicken breast, cube of coconut and a chuck of pineapple. **Use an animal safe skewer.**

RAINBOW CHOP

Ingredients: (Adjust ingredients as required)
Finely grated cauliflower and carrots, finely chopped green chilli, cooked and diced yellow squash, finely chopped broccoli, finely chopped sweet peppers, cooked Quinoa and human grade organic almonds.

Mix all ingredients in with cooked Quinoa. Chop or grate 1-2 organic human grade almonds and sprinkle on top. **Do not leave in the cage more than one to two hours.**

COUSCOUS SALAD

Ingredients: (Adjust ingredients and quantities as required)
Couscous, butternut, 1 okra, kale, chilli peppers, 1 tsp chopped human grade walnuts and raw broccoli.

Cook couscous as you would do for yourself. Steam butternut until tender and chop finely. Finely chop remaining ingredients and mix all in with the couscous.

GREEN DAY CHOP

Ingredients: (Adjust ingredients as required)
Sprouted Microgreens and sprouted legumes. Finely chop green beans, finely chopped chard, par-boiled peas, cooked brown rice, chopped macadamia nuts and chia seeds.

Mix all together. Sprinkle 1-2 tsp of finely chopped macadamia nuts and chia seeds on top. **Do not leave in the cage more than one to two hours.**

SWEET POTATO AND CARROT FRITTERS

Ingredients:
1 medium sweet potato, peeled and grated
200g carrots, peeled and grated
2 red chillies, finely chopped
4 tbsp plain flour
3 free-range eggs, beaten
1 tsp organic extra virgin coconut oil
Cayenne pepper

Preheat oven to 200°C for fan oven. Squeeze the liquid out of the potato and carrots and place in bowl with chopped chillies. You can season with a little cayenne pepper. Add the rest of the ingredients and mix together.

Grease a baking tray with coconut oil. Mould the mixture into round patties. Coat the patties with a little coconut oil and cook for 20-25 minutes or until golden. Serve cool or just warm. **Quick tip: The more liquid squeezed out the veggies, the crispier the fritter.**

VEGGIE OMELETTE

Ingredients: (Adjust ingredients as required)
1 tsp half fat butter
100g frozen peas
¼ courgette, chopped
¼ red pepper, chopped
¼ yellow pepper, chopped
¼ green pepper, chopped
2 red chilies
A dash semi skimmed milk
30g of grated cheddar cheese
4 free-range eggs

Sauté the peas, peppers, courgette and chillies in the butter for a few 3-5 minutes. Whisk eggs, milk and cheese together. Pour over the veggies and cook until golden brown underneath. Then place under the grill for another 5 minutes and **serve warm, not hot**. Garnish with parsley.

FIVE GRAIN CHOPPED SALAD

Ingredients: (Adjust ingredients as required)
Par-boiled peas, red sweet peppers, chopped chilli, grated pumpkin, finely chopped broccoli and a mixture of healthy cooked grains; spelt, barley, durum wheat, brown rice and oats.

Chop all veggie ingredients together in a food processor, then add to the cooked grains and serve cool. **Remove from cage within two hours.**

A SPRING DAYS CHOP

Ingredients: (Adjust ingredients as required)
Baby courgettes, dandelion greens, brussels sprouts, grated beetroot, pea-shoots, red or green chilli, pomegranate seeds.

Finely chop all ingredients, add pomegranate seeds and mix into chop.

THREE QUINOA SALAD

Ingredients: (Adjust ingredients as required)
Cooked red, black and white quinoa, green chilli, sprouted seed, red cabbage, baby corn, water crest, 2 baby tomatoes chopped.

Chop all veggie ingredients together in a food processor, then add the quinoa and serve cool. **Remove from cage within two hours.**

SUMMER SALAD

Ingredients: (Adjust ingredients as required)
Microgreens, kale, carrots, bell pepper, red chilli, bucket-wheat flakes, sugar snap peas and chopped apple **(remove seeds)**

Finely chop all ingredients, add bucket-wheat flakes and mix together.

BLUEBERRIE FLAPJACK FUN

Ingredients:
Whole wheat pancake mix and blueberries.

Make batter mix as instructed on the box and add blueberries. **When cooked Serve cool. You can freeze these.**

<u>HIDDEN PELLET RECIPES</u>

PUMPKIN VEGGIE BREAD

Ingredients:
2 cups organic pellets
1 ripe peeled banana
6 free-range eggs
6 tbs canned pumpkin (low sodium)
1/3 cup organic extra virgin coconut oil

½ cup apple sauce
2 cups mixed vegetables of your choice.
1 cup cooked brown rice
2 cups cornmeal
1 ½ tbs baking powder
Organic carrot juice

Preheat the oven to 350°C
Mix all wet ingredients together in a food processor. When blended, add the corn meal and baking powder to the mix and stir in well together.

If the mixture is too dry, then add some carrot juice. Pour into a greased pan and bake for 40-50 minutes or until there is no residue on the baking toothpick.

NUTTY CORN BREAD

Ingredients:
2 boxes of corn bread mix
2 large free-range eggs
3 over-ripe bananas, mashed
1 cup ground organic pellets
½ cup ground human grade nuts of your choice
½ cup frozen veggies of your choice
1 cup organic apple or carrot juice

Preheat the oven to 375°C
Mix all dry ingredients together, then add in all wet ingredients and blend all together. Use the apple or carrot juice accordingly to make the mixture smooth. Pour into greased pan and cook for 35-45 minutes or until baking toothpick comes out clean. You can freeze or refrigerate these up to three days.

VEGGIE MAC AND CHEESE

Ingredients:
1 box of macaroni and cheese
½ cup ground organic pellets
¼ cup carrots
¼ cup par-boiled corn
½ cup millet

Make the mac and cheese according to the box instructions; add pellets, carrots, corn and mix together. Sprinkle the millet on top or you can sprinkle seed, which ever gets your bird's attention to try out the food. **Serve warm, not hot. As this is a rich recipe feed in moderation.**

ORGANIC PELLET BALLS

Ingredients:
1 cup organic pellets, ground
½ cup cornmeal
½ cup whole wheat flour
1 cup human grade safe nuts of your choice
4 free-range eggs
2 carrots cooked and pureed
Organic apple or carrot juice

Preheat the oven to 375°C
Mix all the ingredients together, add apple or carrot juice accordingly to mould a firm dough. Roll into balls and place on cookie sheet. Bake for 20-30 minutes. You can roll these in crushed nuts before baking.

SUMMER FUN RECIPES

Q: WHAT FUN FOODS CAN I OFFER MY BIRDS IN THE SUMMER? SOMETHING TO KEEP THEM COOL AND HYDRATED.

A: It is important that parrots keep hydrated in the summer. The very best way of doing this is by making sure their water bowls are regularly filled with cool fresh water. Always watch for signs of heat fatigue in the summer months; look out for symptoms such as the bird holding its wings away from its body, panting, looking fatigued and excessive thirst.

FRIUT SALAD LOLLIES

Ingredients: (Adjust ingredients as required)
Apple- **cored,** grapes, strawberries, **peeled** kiwi, raspberries, water and a lolly stick.

Chop it all up and place in lolly mould, add water till it just covers the fruit, place the lolly stick in and freeze.

BEETROOT BANGER SMOOTHIE

Ingredients: (Adjust ingredients as required)
Peeled beetroot, carrots, kale, spinach, sprig of parsley.

Blend all together and serve. **Use spinach and parsley in moderation.**

STRAWBERRY AND YOGURT POPS

Ingredients: (Adjust ingredients as required)
Strawberries and organic plain yogurt

Dip strawberries in plain yogurt and freeze until the yogurt is set. **Parrots are lactose intolerant so use yogurt in moderation.**

PAPAYA AND MANGO POPS

Ingredients: (Adjust ingredients as required)
Peel the papaya and **remove seeds. (Don't throw away papaya seeds)** Mango **remove pip**. 1 tbsp chia seeds, 1 tsp poppy seeds.

Blend mango and papaya in blender until smooth. Add water or organic coconut water if required. Stir in chia and poppy seeds. Place mixture in lolly moulds and freeze. Sprinkle the papaya seeds on top when serving.

APPLE- PEAR AND KIWI CRUMBLE SMOOTHIE

Ingredients: (Adjust ingredients as required)
Peeled and cored apple, pear- **cored, peeled** kiwi, 3 crushed human grade walnuts.

Blend all together until smooth. Add water or organic coconut water if required. Stir in the chopped walnuts and serve. You can also pour into lolly moulds and freeze for a sorbet.

MELON AND BANNANA POPSTICLES

Ingredients: (Adjust ingredients and quantities as required)

1 small peeled banana	1 cup chopped strawberries
¼ cup watermelon	A few grapes
1 large red apple, cored	1 small peeled orange **(seedless)**
¼ cup honeydew melon	3 human grade pecans
¼ cup cantaloupe melon	

Blend all the fruit ingredients together, then stir in nuts. Pour into ice cube tray, or lolly mould and freeze. This can also be offered as a smoothie.

FRUIT SALAD

Ingredients: (Adjust ingredients as required)
Peeled banana, pear, grapes, strawberries, **peeled** kiwi, **seedless peeled** orange, blueberries, raspberries, cranberries, **peeled** mango **(remove pip)**, blackberries, **peeled** papaya with seeds, **peeled** watermelon.

Chop up coarsely for larger birds and finely for smaller birds. You can sprinkle on top chia seeds, flax seed, pine nuts, chopped human grade nuts, millet or pellets.

WATERMELLON AND BERRY SALAD

Ingredients: (Adjust ingredients as required)
Watermelon, blueberries, raspberries, cranberries, elderberries, blackberries, gooseberries.

Cut watermelon slices out with a shape cookie cutter and add berries.

NUTTY GRANOLA PEAR WEDGES

Ingredients: (Adjust ingredients as required)
A pear cored, a good quality commercial peanut butter, organic sugar free granola.

Cut the pear into wedges. Coat half of the wedge with peanut butter, then roll in granola.

FRUIT KEBAB

Ingredients: (Adjust ingredients as required)
Slice of apple, coconut, pineapple, orange, banana, grape, mango, strawberry. Thread it all onto an animal safe skewer and watch the fun.

WATERMELON AND RASPBERRY SMOOTHIE

Ingredients: (Adjust ingredients and quantities as required)
Watermelon, raspberries, and 1tsp chia seeds.

Blend all together and serve.

MANGO AND PEACH LOLLIES

Ingredients: (Adjust ingredients as required)
Mango, peach, sprig of mint, raw coconut water and a lolly stick.

Remove mango and peach stones; blend all ingredients together, add coconut water as needed. Pop in the stick and freeze in lolly moulds. **Note: Check the label on the coconut water, it has to be free from sugars and preservatives.**

NOTE: When making lollies only use the safe wooden lolly sticks which are designed for the use with food. Large parrots that use their feet while eating can hold the lollies; smaller parrots that do not eat with their feed, you can serve in a bowl or on a plate. Never serve smoothies or lollies in glassware.

WINTER MASHES

There is nothing quite like a delicious winters mash to warm you up and parrots relish them. Below, I will share a few mashes which are favoured by my own flock.

SWEET POTATO AND PUMPKIN MASH

Ingredients: (Adjust ingredients as required)
Peeled and boiled sweet potato, boiled pumpkin, microgreens, fresh sprig of rosemary-finely chopped, finely chopped baby spinach.

Boil sweet potato and pumpkin until tender, mash them together, toss the rosemary and baby spinach and mix in the mash. Serve the microgreens as a garnish. Serve warm.

BROWN RICE MASH

Ingredients: (Adjust ingredients as required)
Cooked brown rice, chopped dill, chopped kale, sprouted beans.

Finely chop up all veggies. Mix the veggies and sprouted beans into the brown rice. Serve warm.

Remove from cage within two hours.

THREE WINTER SQUASH MASH

Ingredients: (Adjust ingredients as required)
Spaghetti squash, delicata squash, acorn squash, chopped radish, sprig of thyme and sesame seeds.

Cook all three squashes and mash them up, add radish and thyme to the mash. Sprinkle over some sesame seeds. Serve warm.

BEETROOT MASH

Ingredients: (Adjust ingredients as required)
Raw beetroot-grated, finely chopped chard, sweet corn raw or par-boiled, sprouted chickpeas, cooked parsnip, cooked swede, cooked yam. Add 1 Tbsp of flax seed to garnish.

Mash the parsnip, swede and yam together, add the beetroot, chard, corn and chickpeas and blend all together. Garnish with flax seed. Serve warm.

EGG AND SWEET POTATO CHOP

Ingredients: (Adjust ingredients as required)
Eggs and cooked sweet potato.

Boil eggs until hard. Steam sweet potatoes until tender.
Finely chop the sweet potatoes and eggs, mix together and serve warm.

Note: Do not reheat this dish. Remove from cage after an hour.

<u>A PARROT'S PARTY</u>

Here are a few recipes you can try at home which are nutritious, delicious, un-fussy and fun. **While the foods in this section are nutritious, some should not be given daily. All treats should be fed in moderation.**

CRISPS AND DIP

THE CRISPS:

Ingredients: (Adjust ingredients as required)
Beetroot, zucchini(courgette), carrot, sweet potato, turnip, parsnip. Add extra virgin coconut oil and cayenne pepper.

Preheat the oven to 400F
Slice all the veggies into thin slices. Toss them all in a bowl with extra virgin coconut oil just enough to coat the slices. Spread them evenly on a baking tray lined with parchment paper and bake for 10 minutes. Flip and bake for another 5-10 minutes until golden. Watch them carefully as they can burn quickly. Remove when cooked and sprinkle a little cayenne pepper on top and serve cool.

THE DIP:

Ingredients: (Adjust ingredients and quantities as required)
1 cup of chickpeas, well steamed, 1 slice of butternut squash, well steamed, 1 chilli pepper, 3 crushed walnuts to garnish.

Drain cooking liquid. Blend all ingredients together in a food processor until a thick paste is formed; you want the paste smooth, not too thick.
If it is too thick add a little water or organic carrot juice until a smooth dip. Garnish with crushed walnuts.

BEETROOT HUMMUS

Ingredients: (Adjust ingredients and quantities as required)
1 cup chickpeas, streamed, 1 boiled, beetroot (cook until soft), 1 chilli pepper, 2 Tbs pumpkin seeds, chopped to garnish.

Drain cooking liquid. Blend all ingredients together in a food processor until a thick paste is formed; you want the paste smooth, not too thick. If it is too thick add a little water until a smooth dip. Garnish with crushed pumpkin seeds.

MANGO SPRING ROLLS

Ingredients: (Adjust ingredients and quantities as required)
A few mint leaves, microgreens, 3 courgettes (zucchini) 1 large carrot, 1 red chilli, ¼ bell pepper, 1 small mango (remove pip)

Cut the carrot, chilli, bell pepper and mango into long thin strips. Use a vegetable peeler to slice the courgettes lengthwise into ribbons (you are going to use these to roll the veg in). Place the vegetables strips, mango and a few microgreens on the ribbons and roll it up. Garnish with some mint leaves.

LETTUCE CUPS

Ingredients: (Adjust ingredients and quantities as required)
Romaine lettuce leaves. Choose one of the following: boiled brown rice, boiled pasta or boiled quinoa, par boiled peas, sprouted seed, 1 well boiled chicken or turkey breast, extra virgin organic coconut oil.

Wash lettuce leaves well. Mix your choice of either brown rice, pasta or quinoa together with the peas and sprouted seed. Spoon the mixture into the lettuce cups. Shred the chicken or turkey breast and place it on top. Then drizzle a little coconut oil over it.

BLUEBERRY SWEET POTATO TREATS

Ingredients:
1 cup of flour (use coconut, quinoa, bucket wheat or almond)
2 cups mashed sweet potato
½ cup mashed blueberries

Mix all ingredients together. Grease a shallow glass baking tray with organic extra virgin coconut oil and bake for 25 minutes at 350 Fahrenheit. Cut into pieces and then flip over for another 10 mins baking. You can alternate between sweet potato and pumpkin or butternut.

BANANA ROLLED PANCAKES

Ingredients: (Adjust quantities as required)

1 box wholegrain pancake mix, bananas, honey, crush 2-3 almonds.

Make your pancakes as directed on the box. Chop up your bananas. Spread a tiny drizzle of honey on your pancakes and add your banana, then sprinkle the crushed almonds over the banana. Roll them up and serve just warm or cool.

Go easy on the honey, a tiny drizzle will do; you do not want the honey dripping on their feathers. Large parrots will love eating these in their feet; for smaller birds you can cut up the pancake into little pieces and serve on a paper plate. **This are a very special treat, feed in moderation.**

POLLY'S DEVIL EGGS

Ingredients: (Adjust ingredients and quantities as required)
Free range eggs, steamed chickpeas, grated carrot, grated mild cheddar cheese and sesame seeds.

Boil eggs until hard. Cut the eggs into halves and remove the yolk (save the yolk). Steam the chickpeas until tender. Add the yolks and carrots and blend all together in a food processor until smooth. Spoon the mixture into the egg halves and top with a little cheese and sesame seeds. **Parrots are lactose intolerant, use cheese sparingly. Alternatively use cottage cheese.**

BANANA BERRY SUNDAY

Ingredients: (Adjust ingredients and quantities as required)
1 peeled banana, ¼ cup blackberries, ¼ cup blueberries, 1 tbsp finely crushed pecan nuts.

To make the sauce: Toss the blueberries and blackberries into a saucepan with a ¼ cup of water. Bring it to the boil, then reduce heat and allow it to simmer for about 10-15 minutes until the fruit is tender.

Mash up the berries to a desired consistency. Cut the banana into chunks and pour the berry sauce over it. Sprinkle the nuts on top, alternatively, roll the coated banana in the nuts. **Serve cool.** You can stick a wooden popsicle stick into the banana for the larger birds to hold in their feet. Thread the treat onto a pet safe skewer for small birds.

It is a very messy treat so be forewarned. If you do not want to use nuts, you can use a healthy seed such as chia, sesame, and poppy.

PUMPKIN ALMOND MUFFINS

Ingredients:
2 cups flour
2tbs sugar
1tbs baking powder
1 tsp salt
1 free range egg
1 cup organic almond milk
¼ cup melted margarine
2/3 cup cooked and mashed pumpkin
¼ cup chopped carrots

Preheat oven to 375°F
Separate the dry and wet ingredients and mix in separate bowls. When well mixed, add the dry to the wet and mix again until well blended. If the mixture is too wet, then add a little more flour; if too dry add a little more milk. Bake for 20-30 minutes or until the baking toothpick comes out clean.

BAKED SWEET POTATO

Ingredients: (Adjust ingredients as required)
1 sweet potato washed and scrubbed, finely broccoli, finely chopped dill to garnish, cottage cheese, chopped walnuts or pistachio nuts.

Bake the potato until cooked. Scoop out the flesh and mix the cottage cheese and broccoli together. Then place the mixture back into the potato skin. Sprinkle the dill and walnuts on top and serve warm.

FOODS FOR BREEDING BIRDS

It is imperative that parrots are fed on a healthy diet while breeding; not only for the welfare of the parents, but for the making of the egg (embryo) to be successful and for the chick's growth and health.

I have listed below a few foods which are highly nutritious and relished before, during and after breeding season.

- Apricots
- Baby food cereal made with water
- Boiled eggs
- Broccoli
- Carrots
- Chard
- Cooked brown rice
- Cooked oatmeal made with water
- Cooked pasta
- Cooked sweet potatoes
- Corn on the cob
- Egg-food
- Kale
- Moist wholegrain bread
- Mustard greens
- Oranges
- Organic baby food
- Organic pellets
- Parsley
- Peas
- Pumpkin seeds
- Sesame seeds
- Spinach
- Sprouted seed
- Walnuts
- Well-cooked beans

NOTE: This list is not species specific. Therefore, ensure you are feeding the correct dietary requirements for your parrot's species.

WEANING FOODS

Weaning is an extremely stressful period in your parrot's life. Weaning should be done in the chick's time (**never force wean a bird**). **Young birds should ALWAYS be weaned onto soft foods FIRST and should NEVER be weaned straight onto solids.**

The chick needs to learn how to manipulate hard foods as their beak will still be soft. One cannot expect them to crack seeds, nuts and pellets days after they have been weaned. Sadly, many birds have slowly starved to death because the owner has acquired a young parrot which has absolutely no idea how to hull seed or eat hard pellets.

A weaning bird should be offered both hard and soft foods. It is important to allow them to forage for seed and pellets as this is how they learn to manipulate food with their beaks. However, soft foods should always be available until such a time the bird is **completely consuming the solid food**, and not just mouthing it (played with it). Furthermore, watch carefully that the bird is actually eating enough solids to sustain itself. **Fresh veggies and fruit should always be available as part of a healthy staple diet.**

I have listed below a few nutritious weaning foods which can be offered to weaning birds.

- Baby spinach leaves
- Brown rice
- Cooked pasta
- Cooked peas
- Fruit mashed/ mashed berries
- Mashed bananas
- Millet
- Oatmeal
- Organic baby cereal
- Organic baby food
- Par-boiled carrots
- Partly dehulled seed/easy to hull seed
- Scrambled eggs
- Sloppy pellets
- Soft corn
- Soft wholegrain bread
- Sprouted seeds
- Veggie mashes

FEATHERIFFIC FOOD

A parrot's outward appearance is a reflection of their internal health. A beautiful plumage can only manifest by feeding a bird a well-balanced nutritional diet... **(You are what you eat).** Do you know that poor feather quality and improper feather colouring can be a sign of malnutrition!
Vitamin D3 is vitally important for a healthy plumage. Get your birds into the sunshine as much as possible; if this is not possible, ensure you buy an avian UV lamp. Specific vitamin supplements maybe needed for some species of parrot; this can be discussed with an avian vet.

<u>The food list below can help facilitate the nutritional needs for a healthy plumage.</u>

- Adzuki beans
- Almonds
- Apricots
- Banana
- Beans
- Blackberries
- Blueberries
- Broccoli
- Butternut
- Carrots
- Cashews
- Cherries
- Dandelion
- Eggs
- Grapefruit
- Guava
- Honey
- kiwi
- Leafy greens
- Lentils
- Mango
- Papaya
- Parsley
- Pine nuts
- Pomegranate
- Spinach
- Sprouted seeds, nuts, beans, legumes.
- Squash
- Sunflower seeds /soaked and germinated.
- Sweet peppers
- Sweet potato
- Tuna
- Walnuts
- Wholegrains

NOTE: This is not an exhaustive list.

IMMUNE SYSTEM BOOSTING FOODS

A bird's immune system can be compromised by several factors such as toxicities, dietary deficiencies, water deprivation, sudden changes in temperature, ill health, stress, poor living conditions and over-use of certain medications. A nutritional diet is vitally important to help support the immune system, especially during stressful periods.

The foods listed below can help boost the immune system.

- Almonds
- Banana
- Berries
- Boy choy
- Brazil nuts
- Broccoli
- Brussel sprouts
- Cabbage
- Carrots
- Cashews
- Cauliflower
- Cayenne pepper
- Ceylon cinnamon
- Chia seeds
- Chilli peppers
- Dark leafy greens
- Dates
- Eggs
- Fennel
- Figs
- Ginger
- Yogurt
- Honey
- kale
- Kiwi
- Melon
- Oats
- Oranges
- Papaya
- Pecans
- Poultry
- Quinoa
- Sesame seeds
- Spinach
- Sprouted seeds
- Squashes
- Sunflower seeds sprouted/germinated
- Sweet peppers
- Sweet potatoes
- Turmeric
- Walnuts

NOTE: This is not an exhaustive list.

FOODS TO FEED DURING MOULTING AND FEATHER PLUCKING PERIODS

According to Dr Tony Gestier at Vetafarm Australia; feather production requires around 2 ½ to 3 times more energy than egg production. If the bird is not on a nutritional diet during this period, its body will use up any nutrients reveres it has to produce the feathers. This of course means that a bird's plumage quality will suffer, and the bird can experience prolonged moults, as well as abnormal moults. (Gestier, Vetafarm, 2014)

If your bird has started feather plucking a vet exam is needed straight away. Many avian illnesses and deficiencies can cause feather plucking. One should never change a bird's diet or assume it is a behavioural issue without a veterinarian consult being conducted first.

The foods listed below can help facilitate a bird's nutritional needs during moulting and feather plucking periods.

- Almonds
- Apple
- Apricots
- Banana
- Berries
- Brazil nuts
- Broccoli
- Carrots
- Cauliflower
- Collard greens
- Corn
- Cucumber
- Dandelions
- Dark leafy vegetables
- Eggs
- Fennel
- Figs
- Flax seeds
- Ginger
- Hazel nuts
- Honey
- Kale
- Kiwi
- Mango
- Melon
- Mustard greens
- Okra
- Parsley
- Peaches
- Pears
- Plums
- Pomegranate
- Radishes
- Sprouted-legumes
- Sprouting
- Sweet potato
- Swiss chard
- Tomato
- Tropical fruit
- Turnips
- Whole grains
- Winter squashes

FOOD IDEAS FOR ELDERLY PARROTS

As a parrot gets older, they may start to prefer much softer foods. You may notice some elderly birds dip their food in their water bowl trying to soften it a little. Unfortunately, by dipping their food in their water makes it a breeding ground for bacteria and fungus to grow. Therefore, it is important that elderly birds have a choice of both soft and hard foods. You can supply some pellets hard and some soak first for a minute or two in warm water; making them just a little tender **(Note: damp pellets do go sour, so remove them daily)**

Offer lots of different types of mashes served warm, such as pumpkin, butternut, winter squashes, brown rice, and scrambled eggs. There are a few recipe mashes in this book which will be relished. Mashed fruit or soaked fruit such as figs and dates will be appreciated. Smoothies and juices will be a hit, as well as soups served warm. Let us not forget about sprouted and soaked seeds, nuts, grains, and legumes which are highly nutritious and soft enough to be eaten without effort.

It is extremely important that elderly parrots receive the correct nutrients they need at this stage in life. Many start developing aliments which come with age, however, with the correct nutrition many of these aliments can be controlled or perhaps eliminated altogether. It is important for elderly birds to be checked with an avian vet every 6 months; for their weight to be recorded daily and their environment conditioned and controlled accordingly.

FEEDING A SICK BIRD

When a bird is sick, they will often have a poor appetite. The parrot will go downhill very quickly if it does not eat. Their very fast metabolism has to be fuelled in order for the bird's body to function well. Unless told otherwise by your avian vet, feed the sick bird all its most favourite foods. You do not need to be concerned about the calories at this time.

A sick bird may be too weak to hull its own seed; you can help him by rolling over the seed with a rolling pin. You can also offer veggie mashes severed warm, millet, cooked oats, plain digestive biscuits, sprouted seed, organic baby food and cereal, pet shop treats and egg food. If your bird is not interested in anything you offer, your vet may have to feed via a feeding tube, or he may instruct you to feed an adult food supplement orally. **If your bird has not eaten anything you have tried within 24 hours, speak to your vet to assist you or your bird's condition may rapidly decline.**

PARROT FEEDING MYTHS DEBUNKED

A parrot will only eat what his body needs. A parrot in the wild may instinctively eat what its body needs at certain seasons. However, a captive bird has not learnt this and depends on what we feed them to be safe and nutritious for them to remain healthy.

Parsley is toxic to parrots. False. It is rich in many vitamins and minerals. However, as it contains oxalates, it should be fed in moderation.

Sunflowers are highly addictive. Sunflower seeds are not addictive. However, the cracking sound that they make when opened, is often what is addictive to a parrot. Parrots use them as boredom breakers too, keeping themselves entertained.

Large birds should be fed money nuts. Peanuts in the shell should never be fed to birds. Peanuts harbour mycotoxins and aflatoxins, feeding them can cause Aspergillosis.

Feeding fruit and vegetables can give my bird diarrhoea. This is not true; many inexperienced parrot owners confuse diarrhoea with polyuria. Polyuria is whereby the bird passes excess urine. Feeding wet foods such as fruit and vegetables can result in the bird passes excess water in their droppings.

Large parrots cannot eat small seeds, such as canary seeds. Untrue; many large birds relish small seeds. It is fascinating watching huge beaks de-husk such a tiny seed. Give it a try.

Millet can be fed solely as a food source to small birds such as budgies. No food should be feed as a soul source of nutrition. While millet is rich in many vitamins and minerals, it should only be fed as a treat.

Small parrots such as budgies only need to be fed seed. If any parrot species regardless of size is fed a seed only diet, they will become very unhealthy and develop many health concerns.

You do not have to feed your bird fruit and vegetables if they are on a pelleted diet. While pellets are rich in many nutrients, they do not contain all the vitamins and minerals etc that a parrot needs to remain healthy. There is no manufacturing company in the world that can provide all the nutrients a bird needed in a single pellet. A well-balanced diet requires the bird to eat a wide range of foods to help prevent nutritional deficiencies.

A newly weaned chick should be introduced to hard foods such as seeds and pellets immediately once weaned. Sadly, this is one reason why so many chicks run into health issues and often slowly die of starvation unbeknown to the owner. A bird's beak is still very soft when they so young; furthermore, they still need to learn how to manipulate food in order to crack it, grind it or de-hull it. Newly weaned parrots should firstly be introduced to soft mashes, sloppy pellets and easy to hull or soaked and sprouted seeds.

Feeding poultry to parrots makes them cannibals or makes them aggressive. Feeding chicken to a parrot makes them no more a cannibal than humans eating pork. They are not eating a bird of the same species. There has been no documented evidence known to the author to date of publishing this book that feeding a parrot meat or poultry makes them aggressive.

Never feed a parrot the yolk of an egg. This is not true; egg yolks are highly nutritious and contain choline which helps to improve brain and liver function.

Some parrots can eat avocado. There are a few recorded cases where an owner has fed certain species of parrot's avocado without any ill effects. However, it is one of those situations where a professional will scream "Do not try this at home folks!" Avocado is highly toxic to parrots and countless birds have met a horrific painful death after consuming them. So, **NEVER** feed your bird avocado in any form.

Sharing junk food with your bird helps you to bond. It is true that sharing food with your bird will strengthen your bond. However, sharing junk food with a parrot is purely irresponsible. The high fat, sodium and sugar content in junk food can cause the bird to suffer from many ailments such as liver disease, obesity, and diabetes. Instead, share healthy nutritious foods and drinks with your bird.

Parrots should never be fed apple seeds. This is a very controversial subject. Many say apple seeds are toxic to parrots; while in theory this is true, apple seeds do contain cyanide. However, many avian experts have agreed that a bird would have to feed a large amount per day to have any toxic effects. Many avian vets give the advice NOT to feed apple seeds to parrots. Therefore, I would recommend that you to speak to your avian vet FIRST for advice on this matter before offering any apple seeds to your birds.

All species of parrot can be fed the same nutrition. This is not true; there are many species of parrot that require more or less of certain, vitamins, fats, and minerals. You would need to speak to your avian vet about the correct dietary requirements for your individual bird.

You should never feed your parrot grit. Parrot hull their seed; therefore, they do not need grit in their diet. However, many avian experts give the advice to add a little grit in a bird's diet as it contains many minerals which are beneficial. Additionally, it does indeed increase the digestibility of a diet. If grit is offered, it should be fed in very small quantities, perhaps a few grains once a week. Speak to your avian vet about supplementing your bird's diet with grit.

Seed and pellets do not go bad as they are dry foods. Unfortunately, many inexperienced bird keepers do believe this myth. Seed and pellets do indeed go rancid, left out in the open they can spoil and go mouldy. All dry food should be in date and stored correctly. Seed and pellets should be given fresh daily.

Elderly parrots should not be introduced to new foods. Sadly, many elderly birds are not given the attention or care they need and deserve. Unless the elderly parrot is on a special diet due to an ailment, there is no reason why they should not be offered new and exciting foods to sample. The same applies to offering them new toys or teaching new words or tricks. You will be shocked at how quickly an elderly bird can learn, and how much they thrive when given these opportunities.

I should feed my pet bird suet in the winter. Suet is made from hard fats; it is fed to wild birds over the winter months to help them keep warm. It is fantastic for wild birds and has no ill effects because they fly miles a day and are able to burn off the excess calories extremely quickly. Captive birds are unable to do this, even in an aviary setting, therefore, they cannot burn off these calories, resulting in many health issues. Never feed a pet bird any foods produced for wild birds; this includes wild bird seed.

SPROUTING FOR PARROTS

This book wouldn't be complete without a quick guide to sprouting. Many parrot owners hear about sprouting for birds, unfortunately, without researching more deeply into it, they may "imagine" it to be this long complex process. However, it is very easy and of course so nutritious.

If you are new to sprouting, it may be an idea to start with sprouting something quick and easy such as mung beans, then work your way up.

Why sprout in the first place? The most simplistic explanation; you are taking a seed, grain, nut or legume and bringing it to life, then feeding it straight to your bird. While in this state, it is super rich in vitamins, minerals, proteins, and antioxidants. The more scientific explanation is when you soak and sprout a seed it undergoes changes and some of the fat content is converted to protein and vitamins.

Before we start looking at the sprouting guide, there are a few important tips we all need to know while sprouting:

1. The only beans which are safe to soak, and sprout are mung beans, adzuki beans and chickpeas. All other bean types would have to be soaked and cooked thoroughly.
2. It is always best to buy organic and preferably (GMO free) seeds, nuts and legumes; these are of high quality and will produce the best healthy sprouts. **The nuts should always be human grade.**
3. **Only sprout in a glass container, avoid plastic!** Plastic is porous and harbours bacteria.
4. The way in which sprouts are made; a warm, dark, damp environment, is the perfect breeding ground for bacteria and mould to grow quickly. Therefore, an antifungal or antibacterial agent should always be used. **Grapefruit seed Extract** has amazing antibacterial and antifungal properties. It is a fantastic product to use during the sprouting process to prevent mould growth.

5. If any point during the sprouting process the seeds bubble or develop a foul smell, throw away the batch and start again. This means they have become rancid and should never be fed to your birds.
6. Before sprouting all items need to be thoroughly rinsed to remove dirt, as well as to remove toxic compounds which are found in some foods, such as **saponin in Quinoa.**

<u>SOAKING AND SPROUTING GUIDELINES</u>

The soaking and sprouting times below are only guidelines. Many factors may influence sprouting, such as temperature, humidity, climate, and freshness of produce.

Grains:

Barley **(un-hulled)** - **Soak time-** 6-8 hours - **Sprout time-** 2 days.
Buckwheat- **Soak time-** 15 minutes – **Sprout time** – 1-2 days.
Millet- **(Un-hulled)** - **Soak time-** 8 hours- **Sprout time-** 2-3 days.
Oats- **(Un-Hulled)- Soak time-** 8-14 hours- **Sprout time-** 1-2 days.
Quinoa- **Soak time-** 2 hours- **Sprout time-** 1-2 days. **(Rinse thoroughly).**
Spelt- **Soak time-** 8-14 hours- **Sprout time-** 1-2 days.
Teff- **Soak time-** 2 hours- **Sprout time-** 1 day.
Wheat grain- **Soak time-** 7 hours- **Sprout time-** 2-3 days.

Legumes:

Adzuki beans- **Soak time-** 8 hours- **Sprout time-** 3-5 days.
Alfalfa- **Soak time-** 4-14 hours- **Sprout time-** 1-2 days.
Clover- **Soak time-** 4-14 hours- **Sprout time-** 1-2 days.
Chickpeas (Garbanzo beans) **Soak time-** 12 hours- **Sprout time** 12 hours.
Lentils- **Soak time** - 8 hours- **Sprout time-** 12 hours.
Mung beans- **Soak time-** 1 day- **Sprout time-** 2-5 days.
Peas **(Whole)- Soak time** 12 hours- **Sprout time-** 2-3 days.

Nuts & Seeds:

Almonds **(Hulled)- Soak time-** 8-12 hours- **Sprout time-** 12 hours.
Cashews- **Soak time-** 2 ½ hours- **Sprout time-** N/A.
Pecan **(Hulled)- Soak time-** 4-6 hours- **Sprout time-** N/A
Walnuts- **Soak time-** 4 hours- **Sprout time-** N/A

Fenugreek seeds- **Soak time-** 8 hours- **Sprout time-** 2-3 days
Flax seed- **Soak time-** 8 hours- **Sprout time-** N/A
Poppy seed- **Soak time-** 8 hours- **Sprout time-** 1-2 days
Pumpkin seeds- **Soak time-**6-8 hours- **Sprout time-** 1-2 days
Sesame seed-**(Un-hulled)** - **Soak time-** 8 hours- **Sprout time-** 1-2 days
Sunflower seeds-**(Hulled or Un-hulled) Soak time-** 2 hours- **Sprout time-** 2-3 days.

NOTE: These foods listed are considered safe to sprout. If you want to sprout items which are not on this list, then please consult with your avian vet or with a qualified avian nutritionist. Many foods are not safe to sprout or will not sprout.

HEALTH TIP: Feed sprouts in moderation and occasionally to hormonal birds/chronic egg layers, and birds suffering with kidney disease.

THINGS YOU NEED TO GET STARTED

- A wide mouth glass Maison jar with a stainless-steel mesh lid. Alternatively, you can use cheese cloth and a rubber band for the lid. (You can also buy sprouting trays and sprouting machines).
- A variety of safe sprouting food.
- Grapefruit seed extract.

THE SOAKING PROCESS

1. Rinse all your items thoroughly before soaking.
2. Place your items in your sprouting jar and fill with warm water, ensure the water is covering the items. **Then add 5 drops of Grapefruit seed extract per litre of clean water. (20-25 drops per gallon).** Let the items then soak in the Grapefruit extract mixture for the recommended soaking time.
3. Once the items have soaked for the recommended time, drain off the soaking water and rinse thoroughly under clean warm water, then allow to sprout.

THE SPROUTING PROCESS

1. **Rinse your items thoroughly 2-3 times per day.** Each time soaking them in a fresh GSE mixture for 10-15 minutes; then drain without rinsing and allow to sprout. **(See point 2 on soaking process for GSE mixture).**
2. Always place your items in a cool dry place to sprout.
3. Harvest the sprouts when they have grown their little roots.
4. Rinse the sprouts thoroughly before offering them to your birds.
5. You can refrigerate any unserved sprouts for 2-3 days. Do ensure they still fresh before feeding.

NOTE: There should never be water left in the jar after draining. Sprouts should never sit in pools of water.

BIBLIOGRAPHY

B.V. L. (2020). *vitamin content of fruit and vegetables* . Retrieved June 2020, from Lenntech : https://www.lenntech.com/fruit-vegetable-vitamin-content.htm

Birdsupplies. (2020). *Signs of parrot malnutrition*. Retrieved June 2020, from Birdsupplies : https://birdsupplies.com/pages/signs-of-parrot-malnutrition

Brue, R. N. (1997). *Avian medicine principles and application* . Lake worth , Florida , United states of America : Wingers publishing, Inc.

Burger, I. H. (1993). *The Waltham book of companion animal nutrition* . Oxford , England, United Kingdom : Pergamon Press Ltd.

Companions, G. (2020). *Important vitamins and minerals for pet birds*. Retrieved July 2020, from Great companions : https://www.greatcompanions.com/product/important-vitamins-and-minerals-for-pet-birds/

Fisher, J. (2014). *Parrot Monk's guide to companion parrot health & safety* . Salt lake city, Utah, United states of America : Living Novel Enterprises, LLC.

Frothingham, S. (2019, May 22). *Does beetroot offer benifits for your skin* . Retrieved July 2020, from Healthline: https://www.healthline.com/health/beetroot-benefits-for-skin

Gestier, D. T. (2014, August 1). *Moulting in cage birds* . Retrieved June 2020, from Vetzone : https://www.vetzone.com.au/Birds/Articles/Article/tabid/1964/ArticleID/380/Moulting-in-Caged-Birds.aspx#.X3XoXi9Q3BJ

Hannis L. Stoddard, I. D. (2018). *Dealing with Vitamin A deficency in birds* . Retrieved July 2020, from Hotspot for birds: http://www.multiscope.com/hotspot/articles/vitamina.htm

Low, R. (2012). *Parrots and finches healthy nutrition* . Mansfield , Notts, England, United Kingdom : Insignis publications .

Morrison, L. (2020). *How the flock do i care for a parrot?* . Berkshire, England, United Kingdom .

Pesticides in our food. (2017). Retrieved June 2020, from Pesticide action network UK: https://www.pan-uk.org/our-food/

Shoemaker, S. (2020, June 3). *All you need to know about figs*. Retrieved July 2020, from Healthline: https://www.healthline.com/nutrition/figs-benefits

Low, R. (2020, May). Cuttlefish bone is not enough. *Parrot Magazine*(268), pp. 21-23.

Moran, L. (2009 , December). Sorting out Vitamin A and the liver's role . *Parrot Magazine* (143), pp. 14-15 .

Moran, L. (2020, July). Cleaning non-organic produce. *Parrot Magazine*(270), pp. 16-20.

Oakley, S. (2019). *Wild foods herbs & spices for birds.*

Funhouse, P. (2019, October 3). *How to soak and sprout for birds* . Retrieved July 2020, from Parrot funhouse : https://parrotfunhouse.com/blogs/parronting-essentials-blog/soaking-and-sprouting-for-birds-with-schedules

Society, A. H (2020). *The five freedoms for animals.* Retrieved June 3, 2020, from https://www.animalhumanesociety.org/health/five-freedoms-animals.

Made in the USA
Middletown, DE
27 June 2022